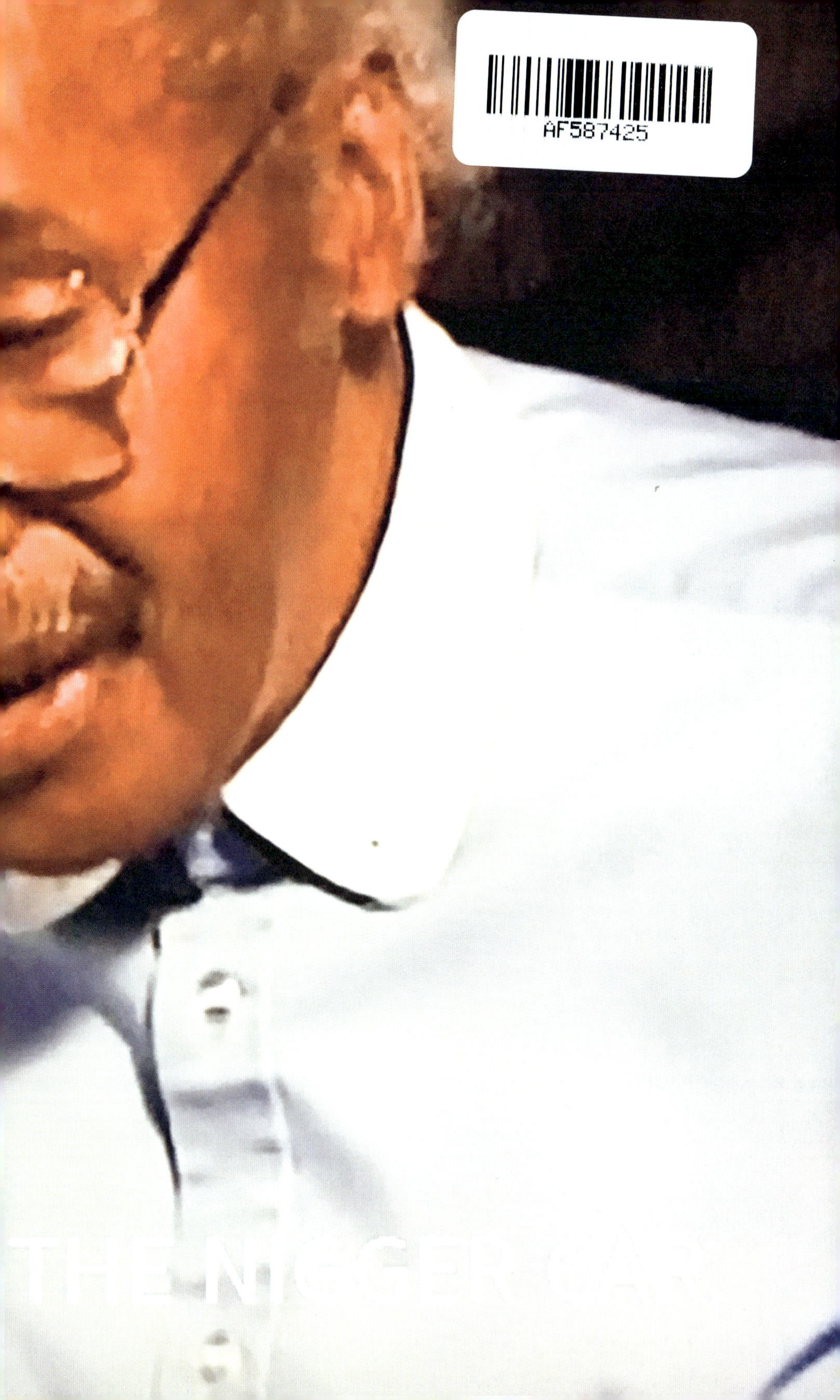

A MISTAKE IS A BEAUTIFUL THING

devin troy strother
yuri ogita

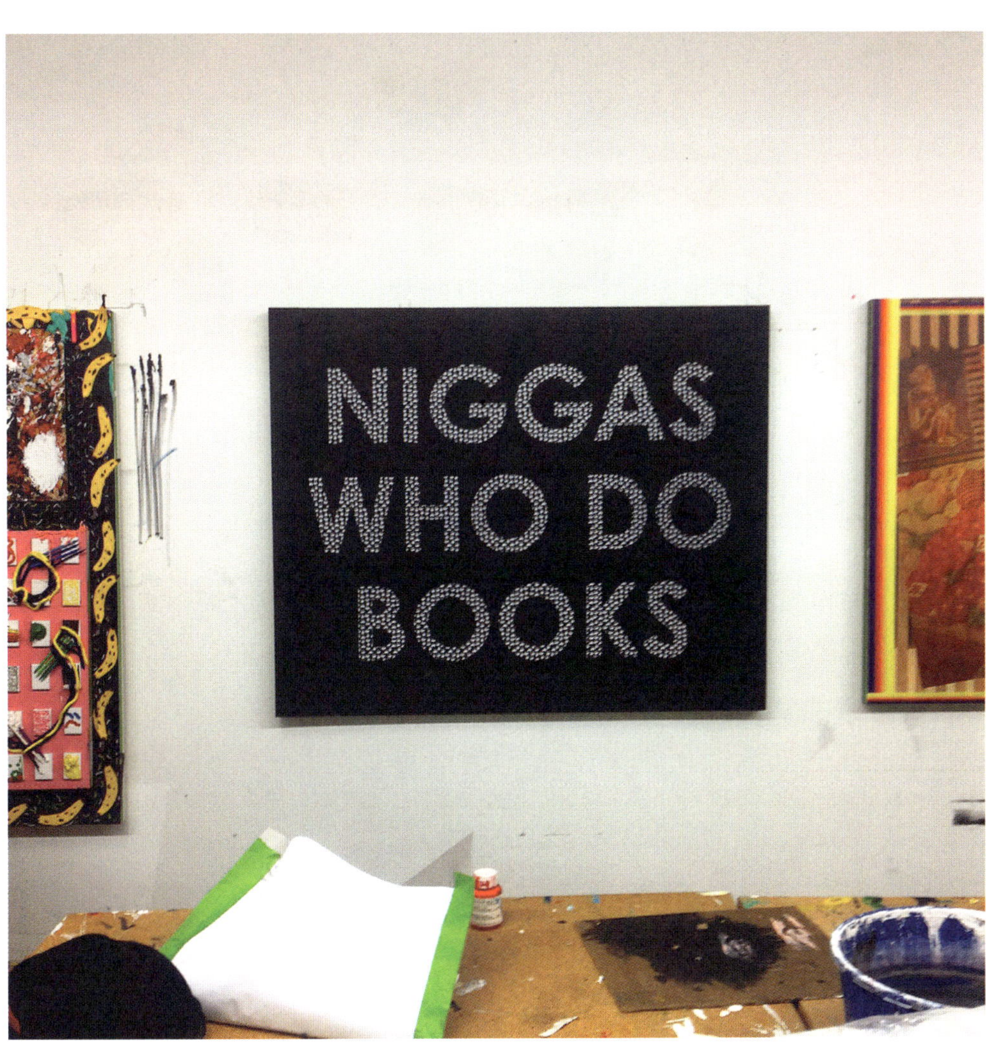

me and you
your momma and your cousin too

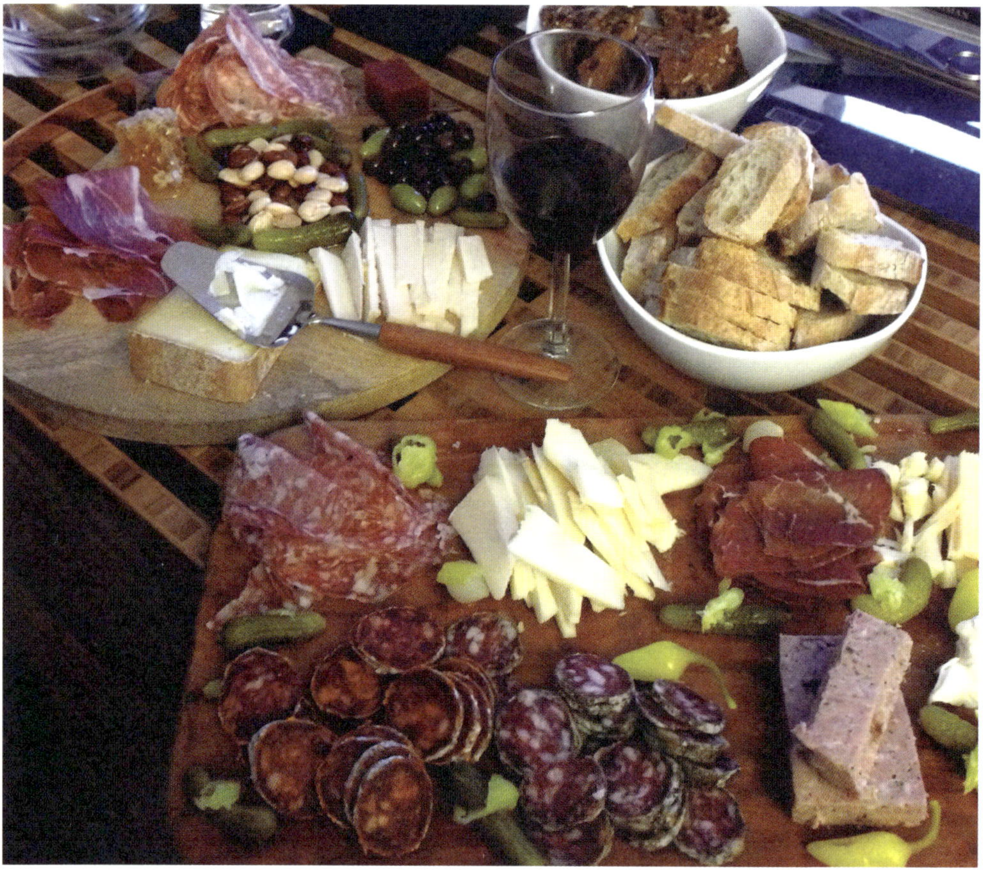

nigga that's just a fancy-ass lunchable

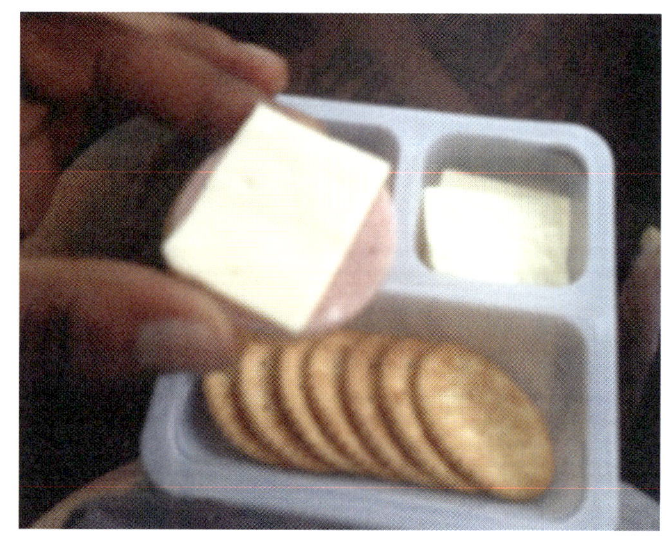

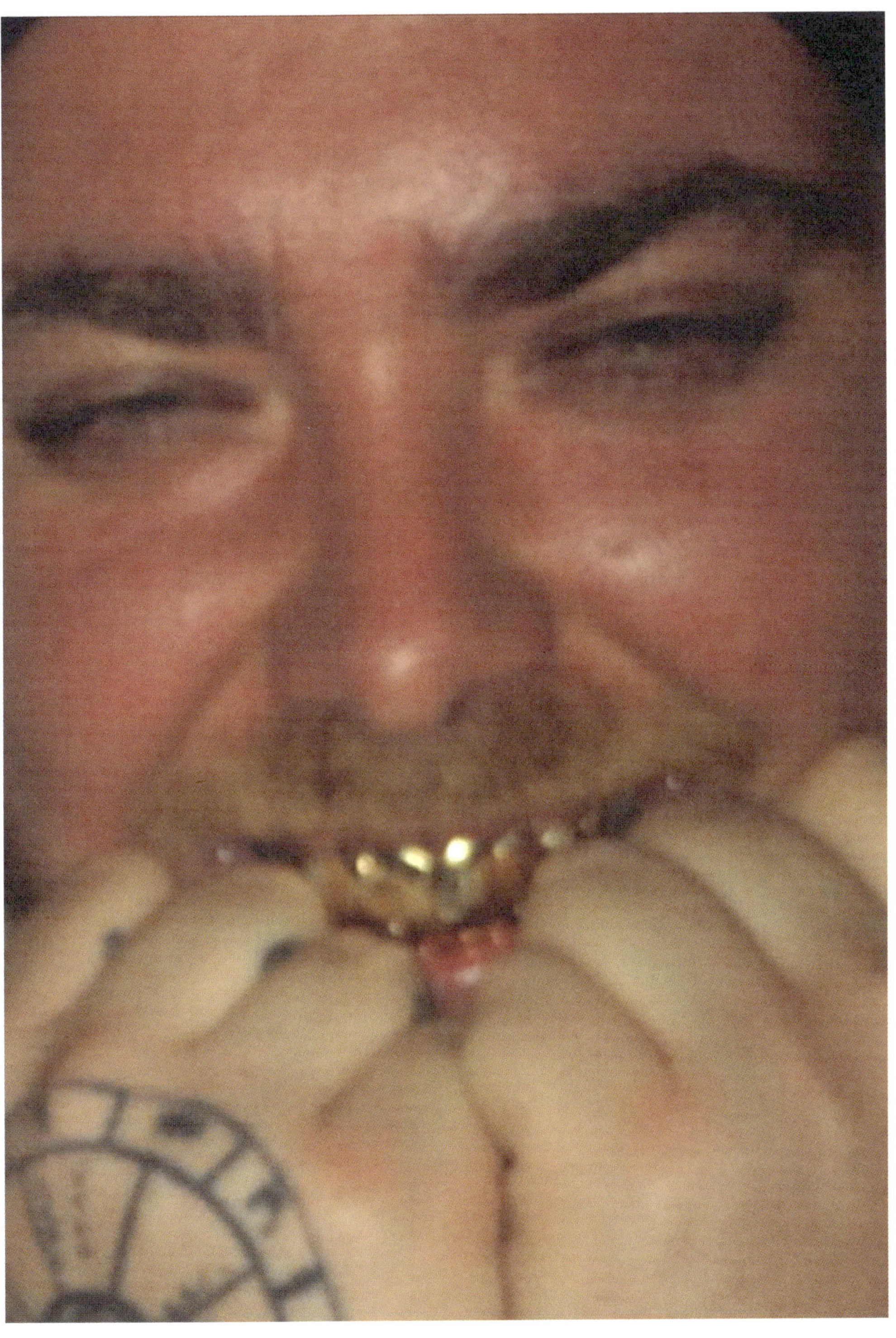

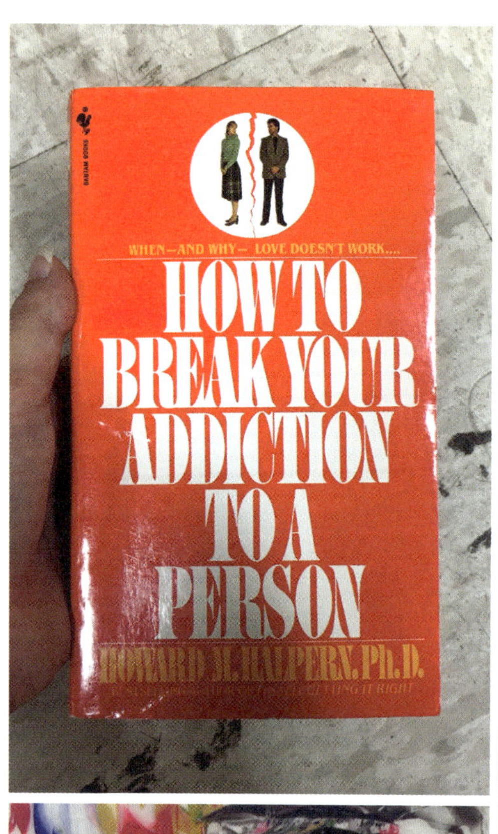
WHEN—AND WHY— LOVE DOESN'T WORK....
HOW TO BREAK YOUR ADDICTION TO A PERSON
HOWARD M. HALPERN, Ph.D.

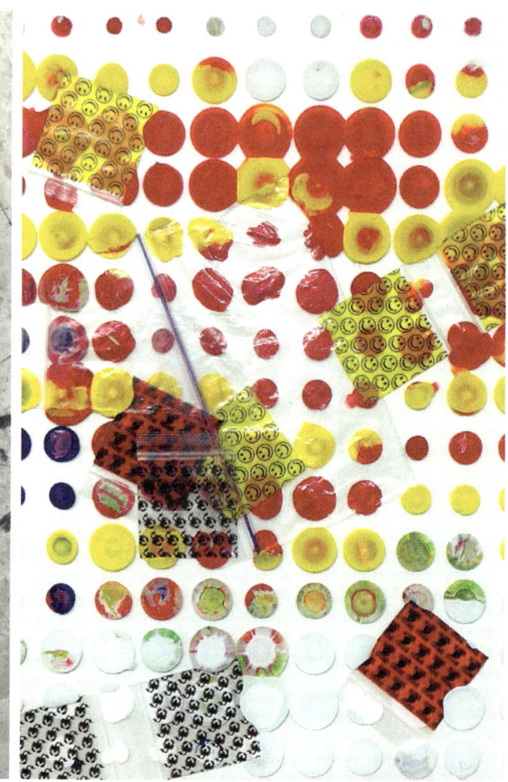

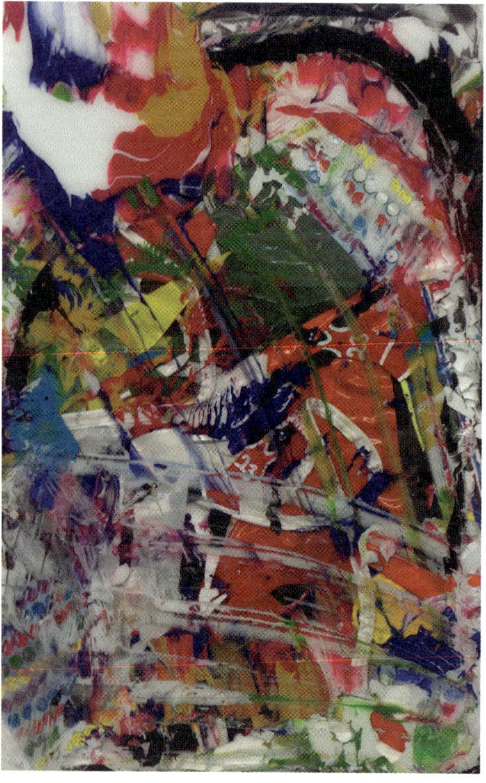

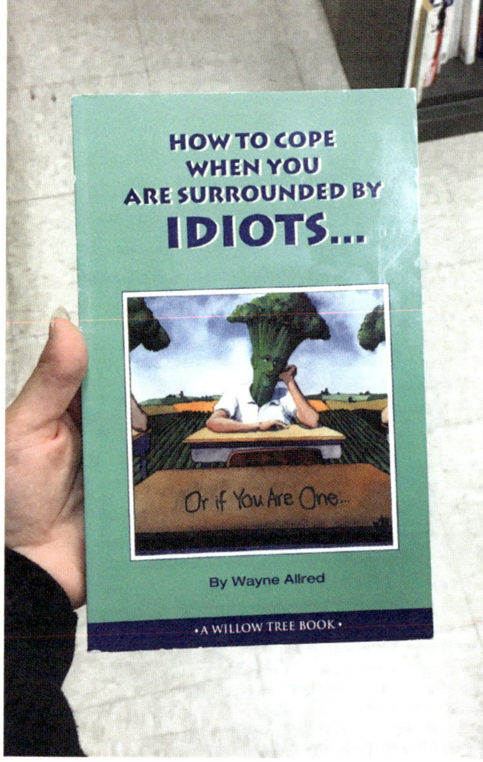
HOW TO COPE WHEN YOU ARE SURROUNDED BY
IDIOTS...
Or if You Are One...
By Wayne Allred
• A WILLOW TREE BOOK •

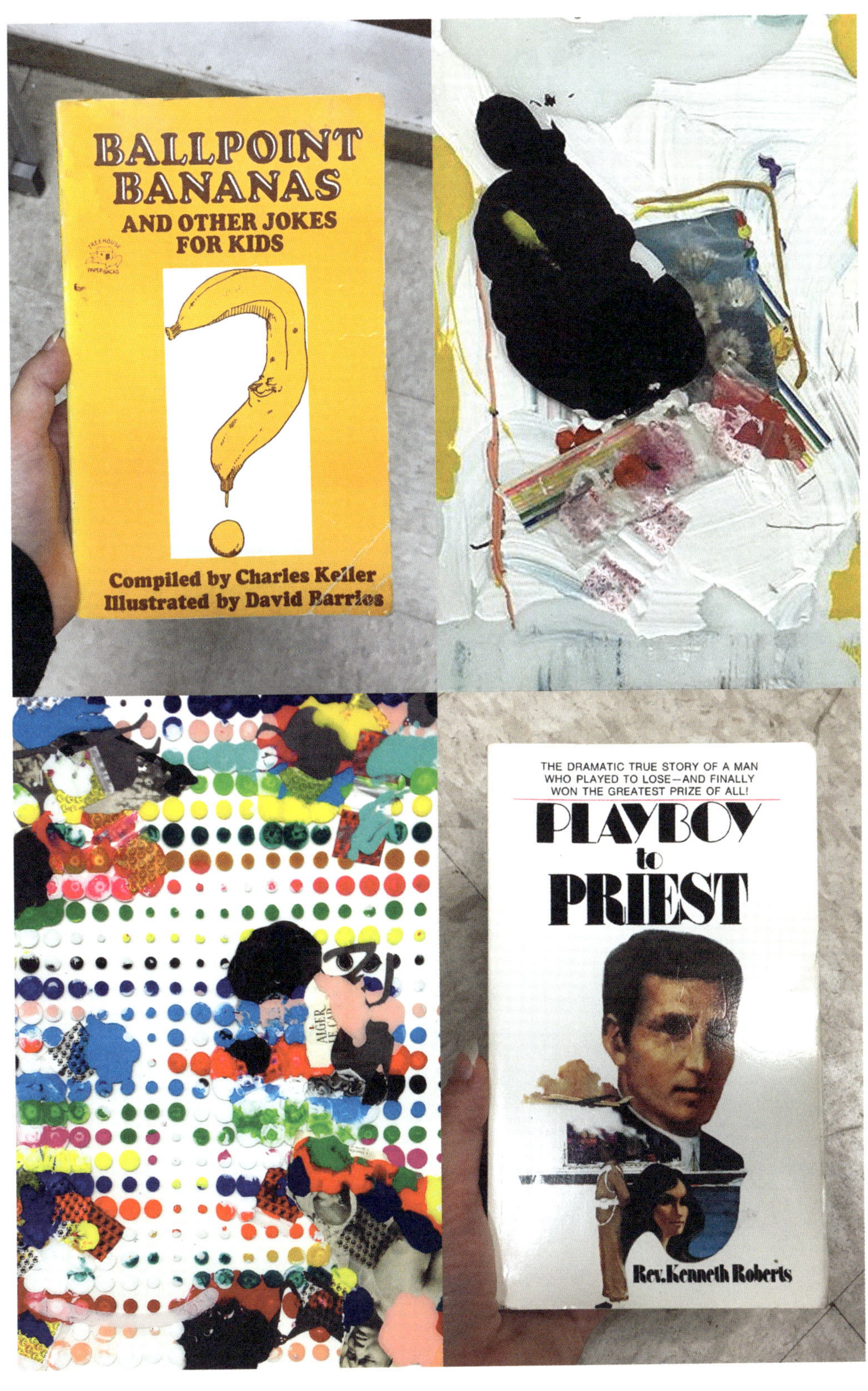
BALLPOINT
BANANAS
AND OTHER JOKES
FOR KIDS
Compiled by Charles Keller
Illustrated by David Barrios
THE DRAMATIC TRUE STORY OF A MAN
WHO PLAYED TO LOSE—AND FINALLY
WON THE GREATEST PRIZE OF ALL!
PLAYBOY
to
PRIEST
Rev. Kenneth Roberts

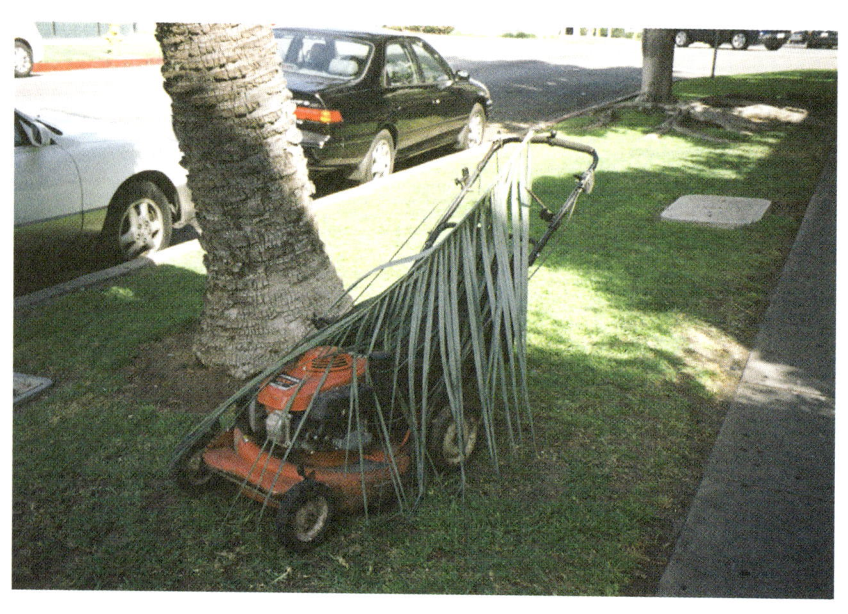

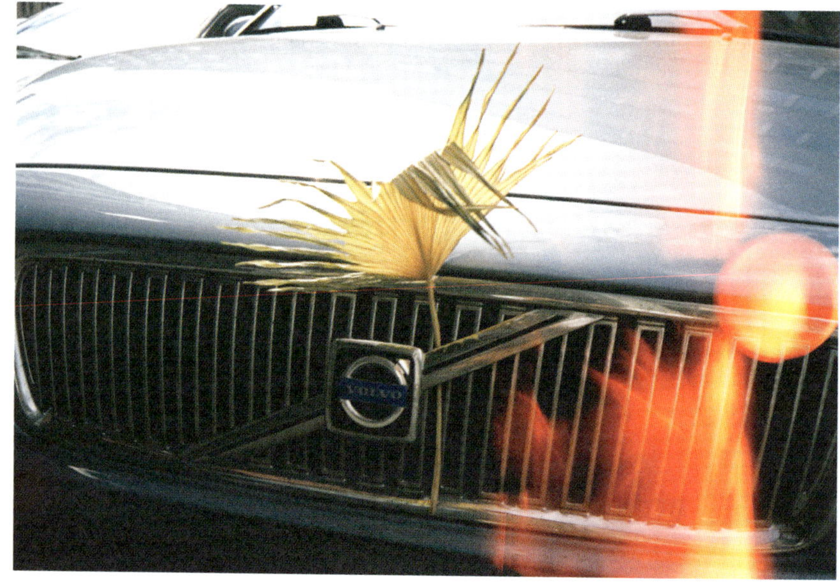

koreatown and köln /
happy now, smile later

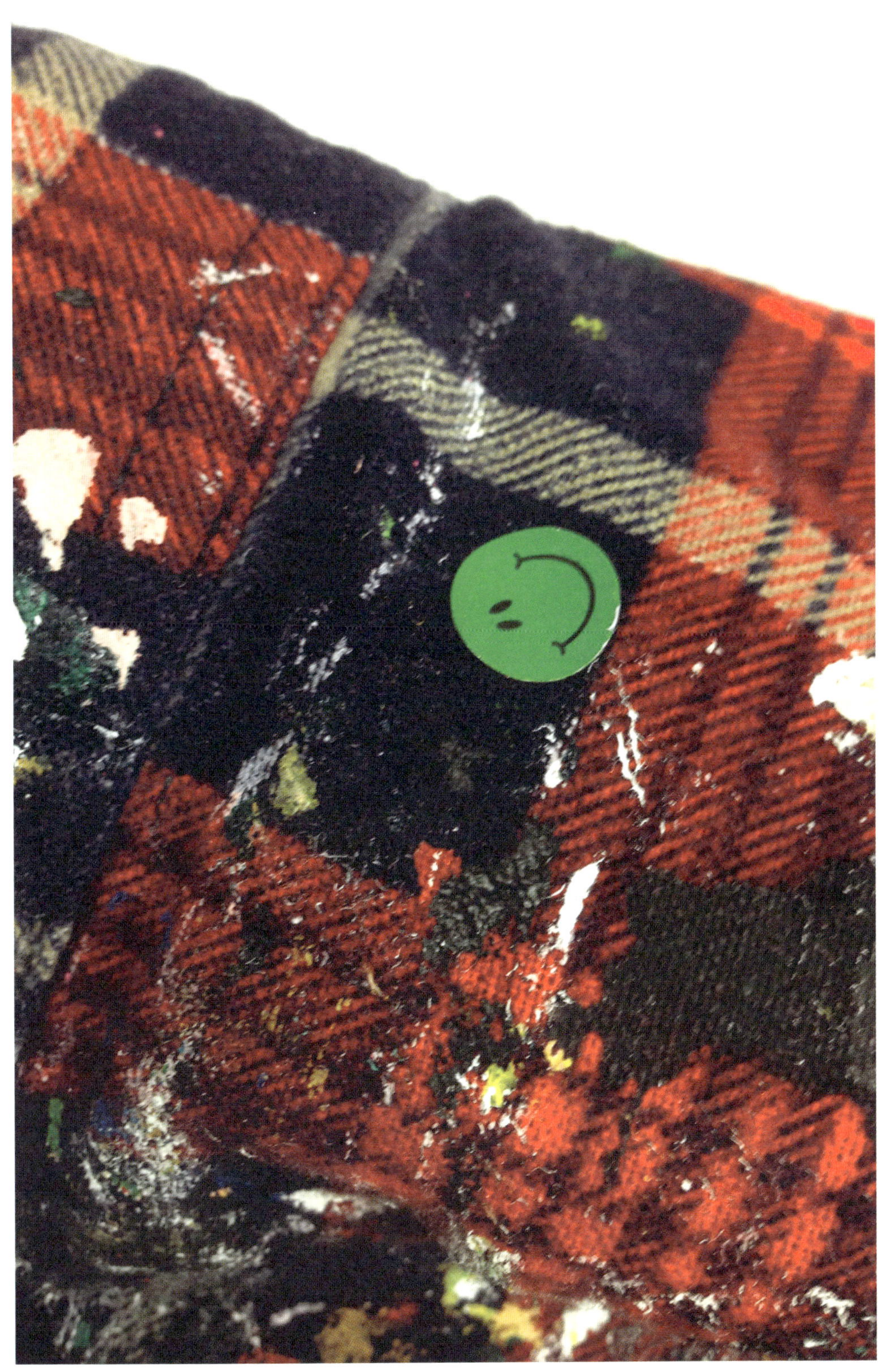

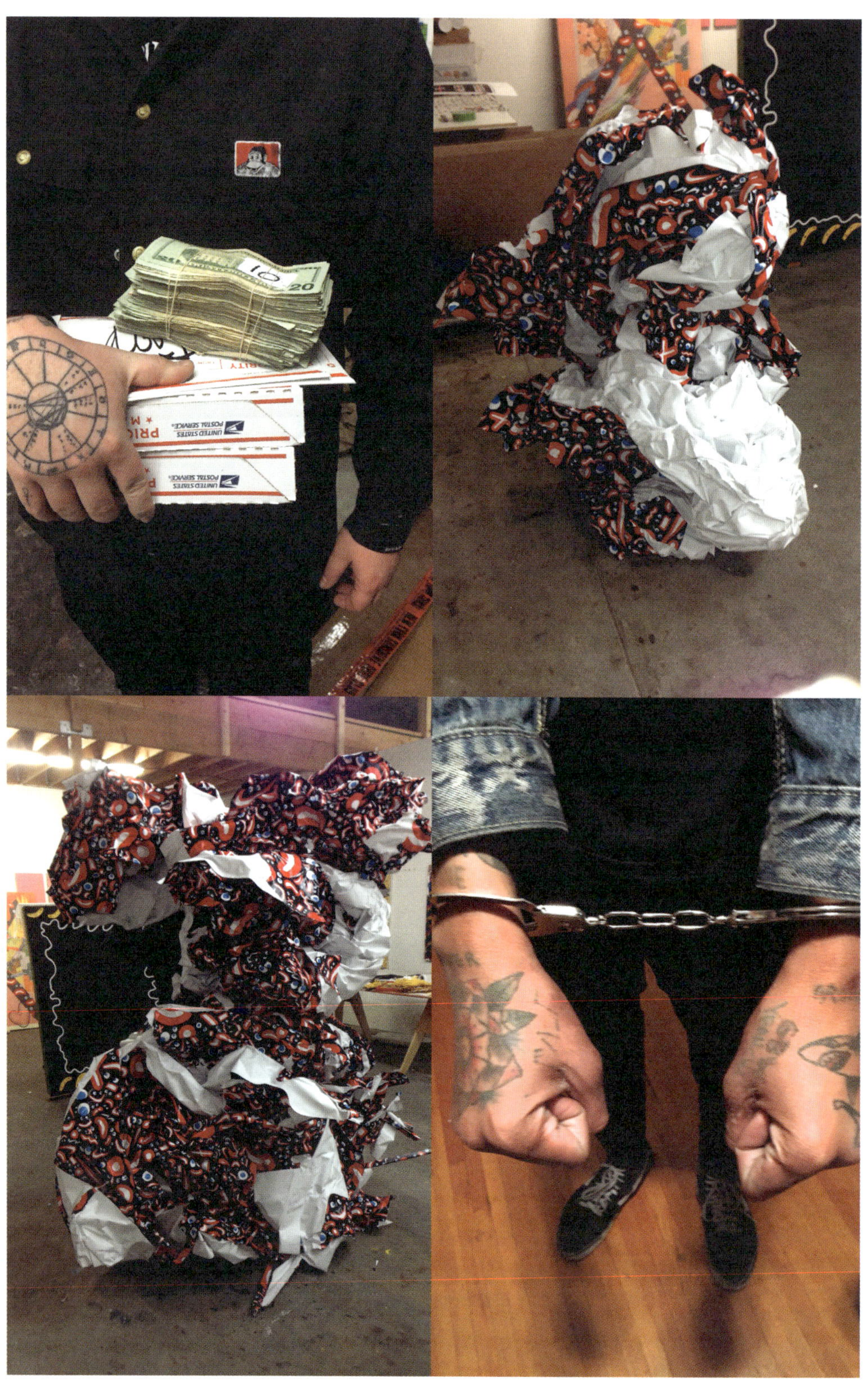
UNITED STATES POSTAL SERVICE
UNITED STATES POSTAL SERVICE

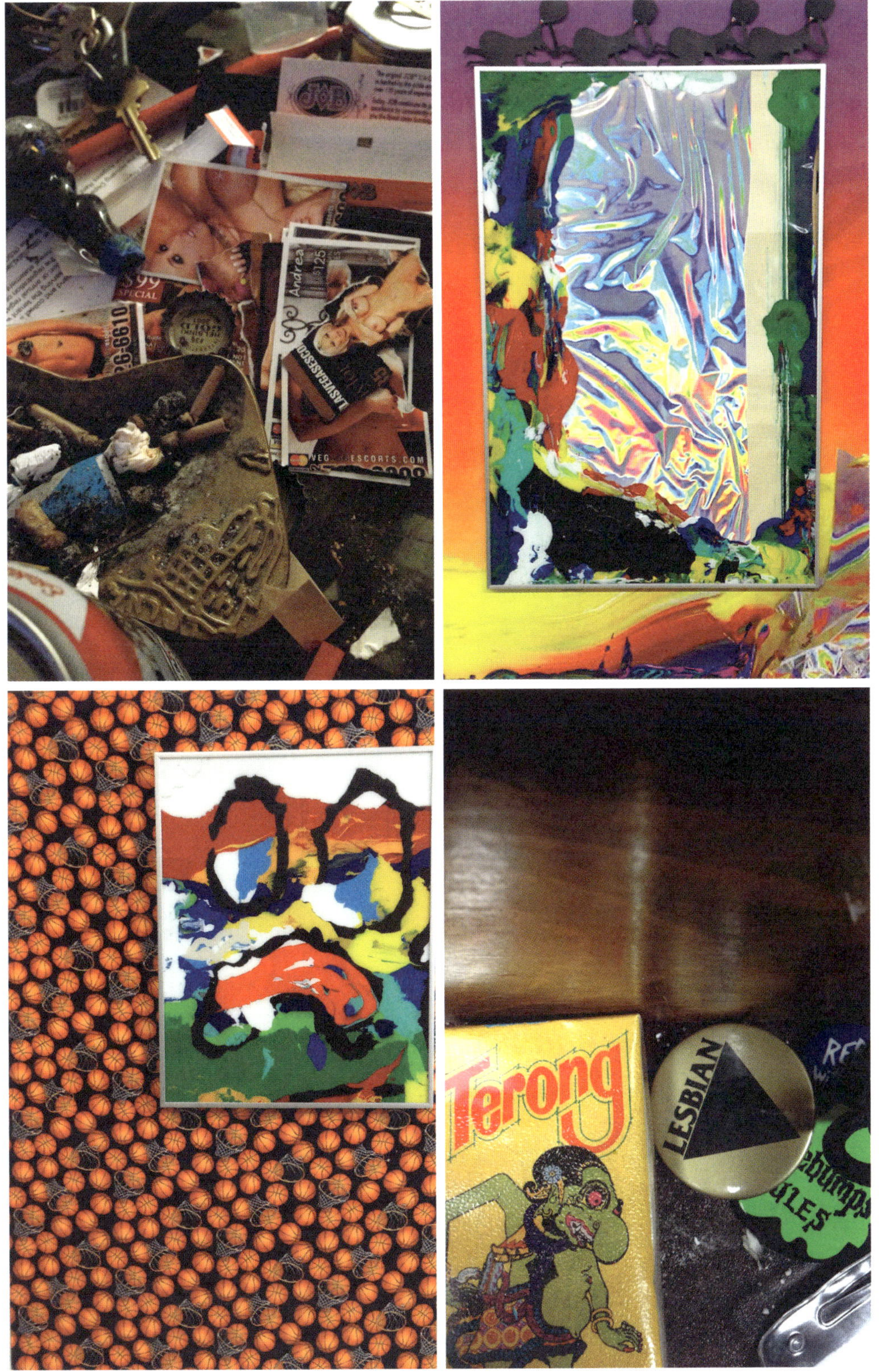
LASVEGASESCO
VEGASESCORTS.COM
Terong
LESBIAN

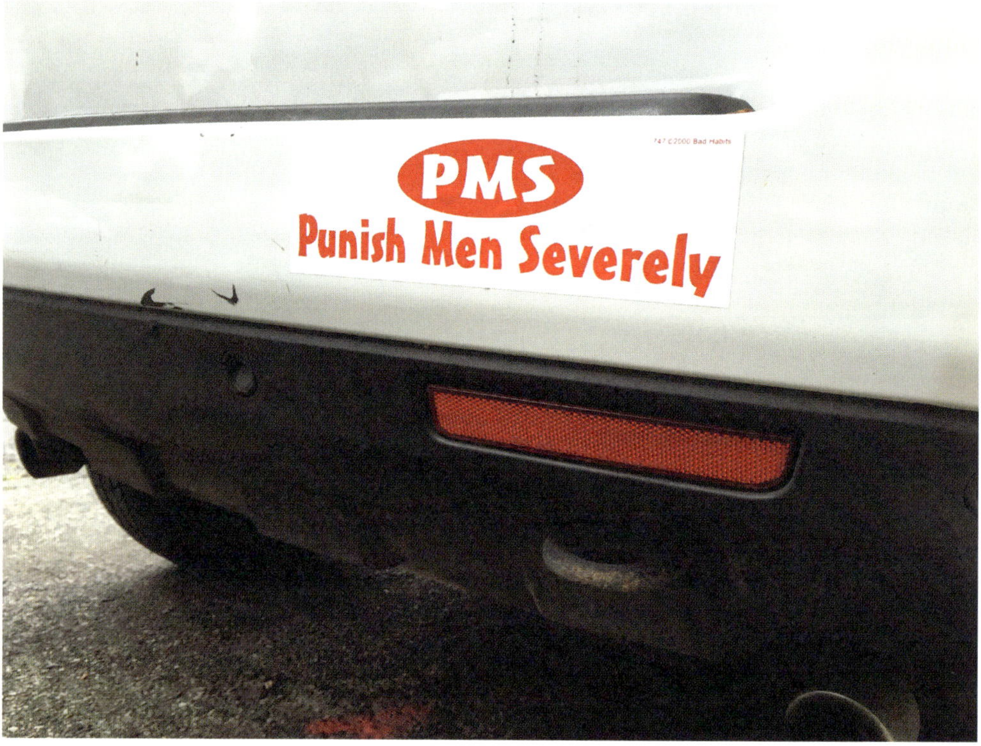

PMS
Punish Men Severely

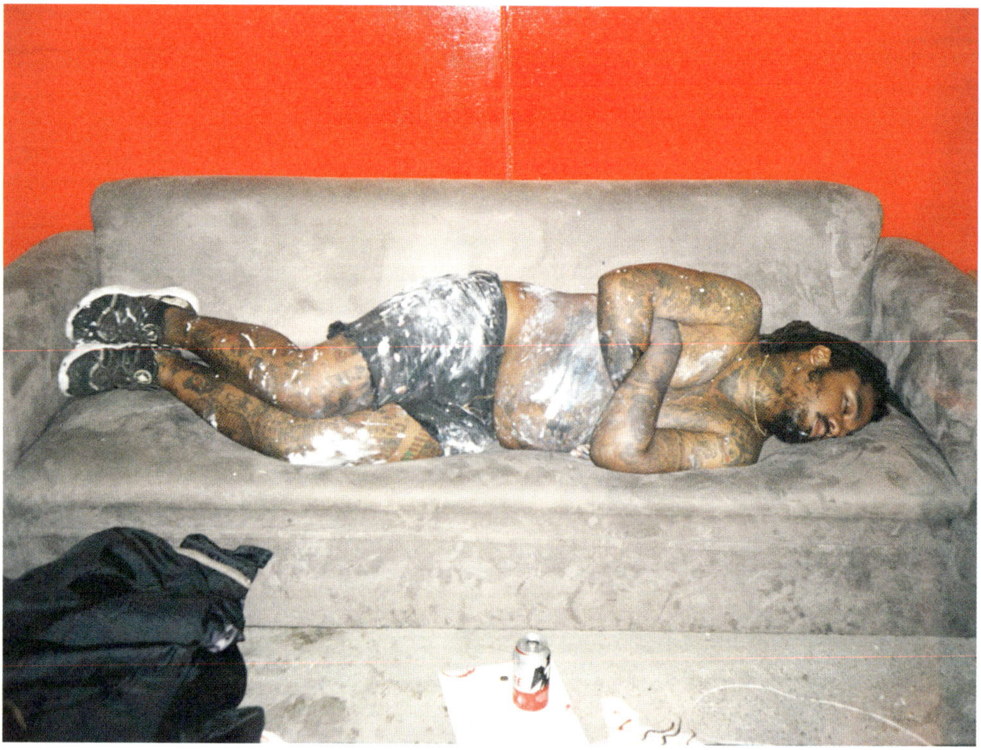

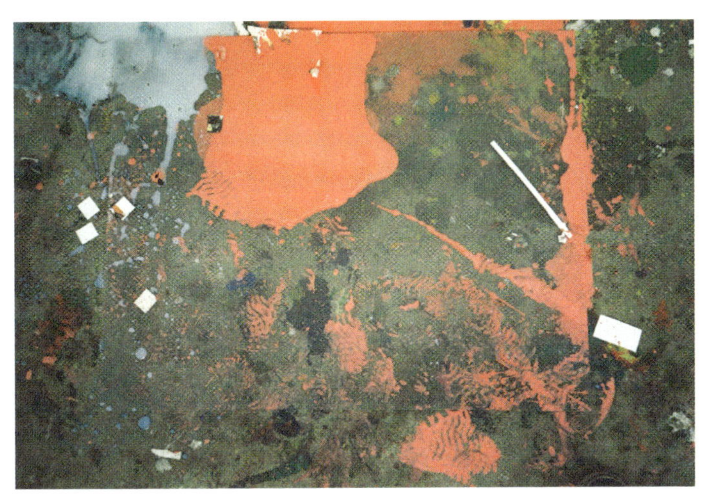

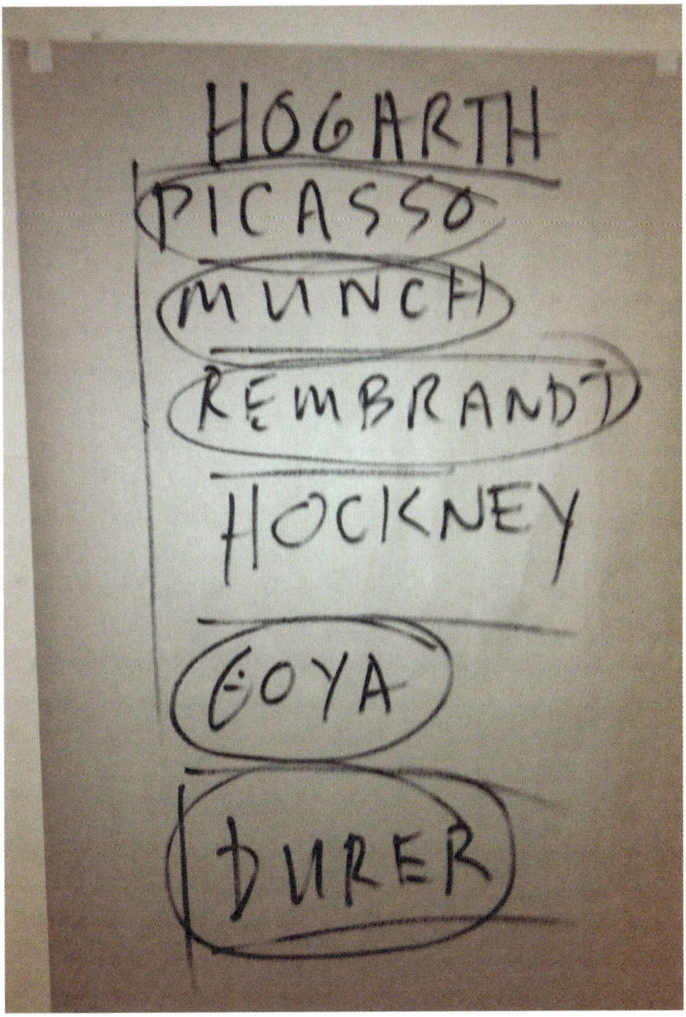

HOGARTH
PICASSO
MUNCH
REMBRANDT
HOCKNEY
GOYA
DURER

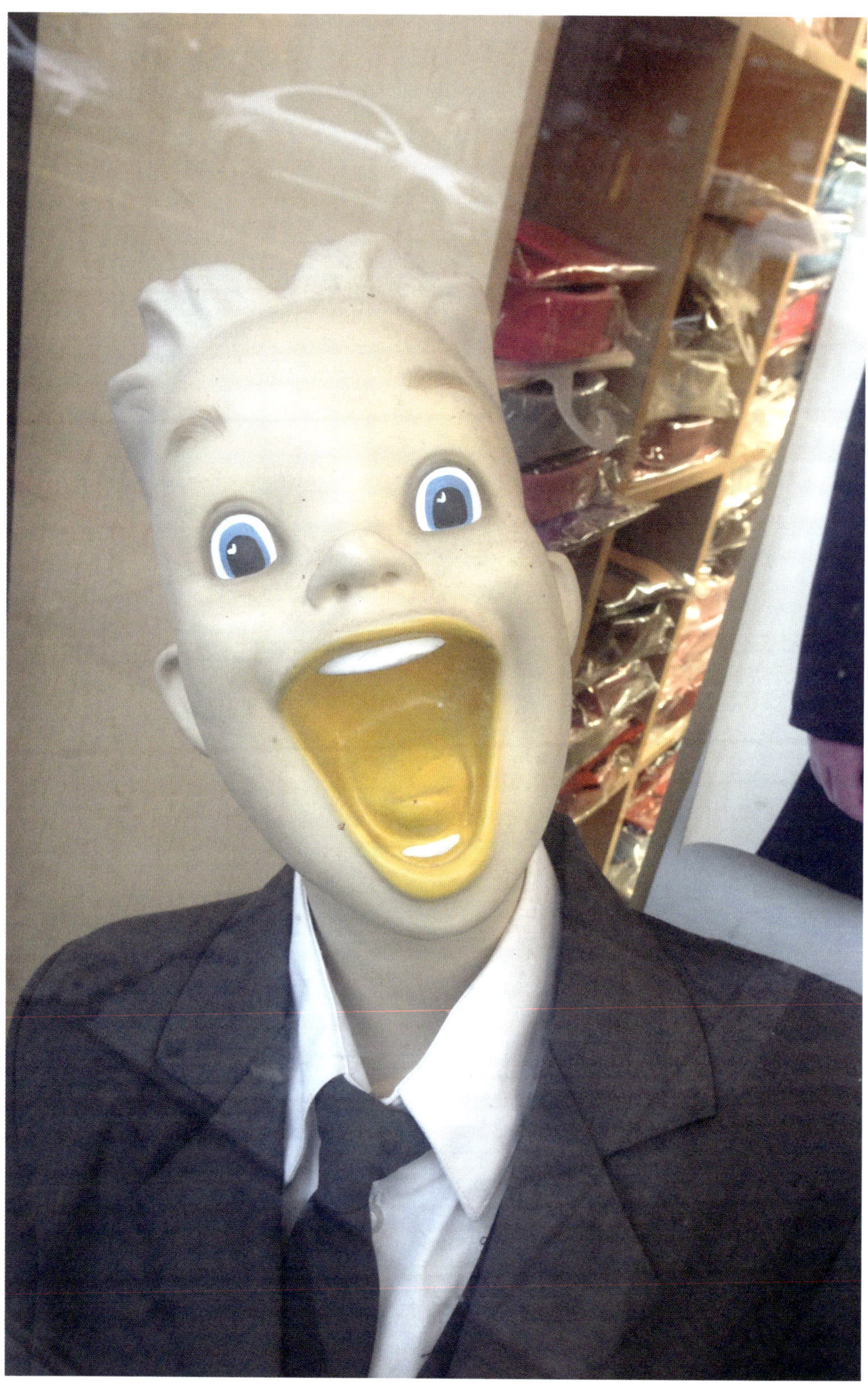

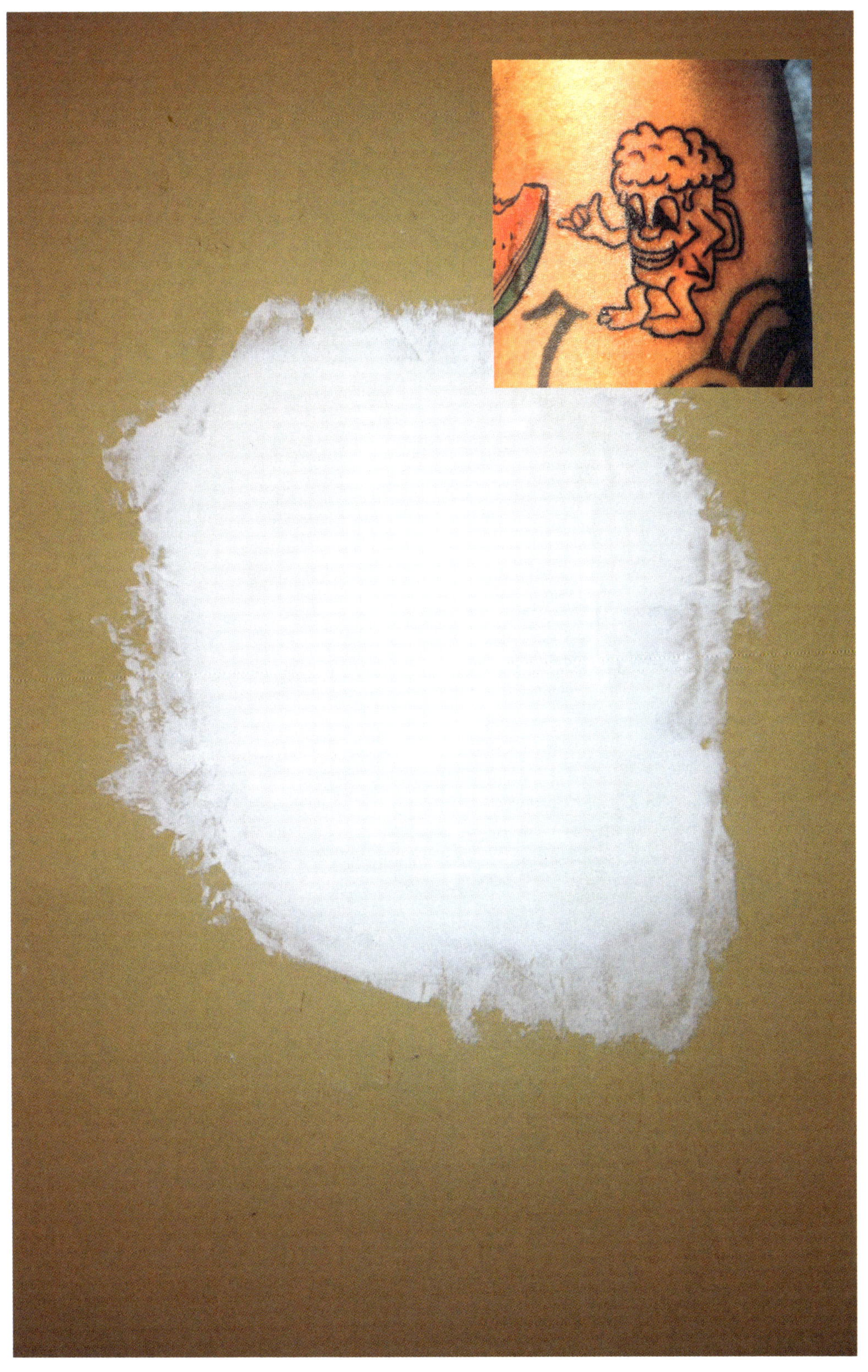

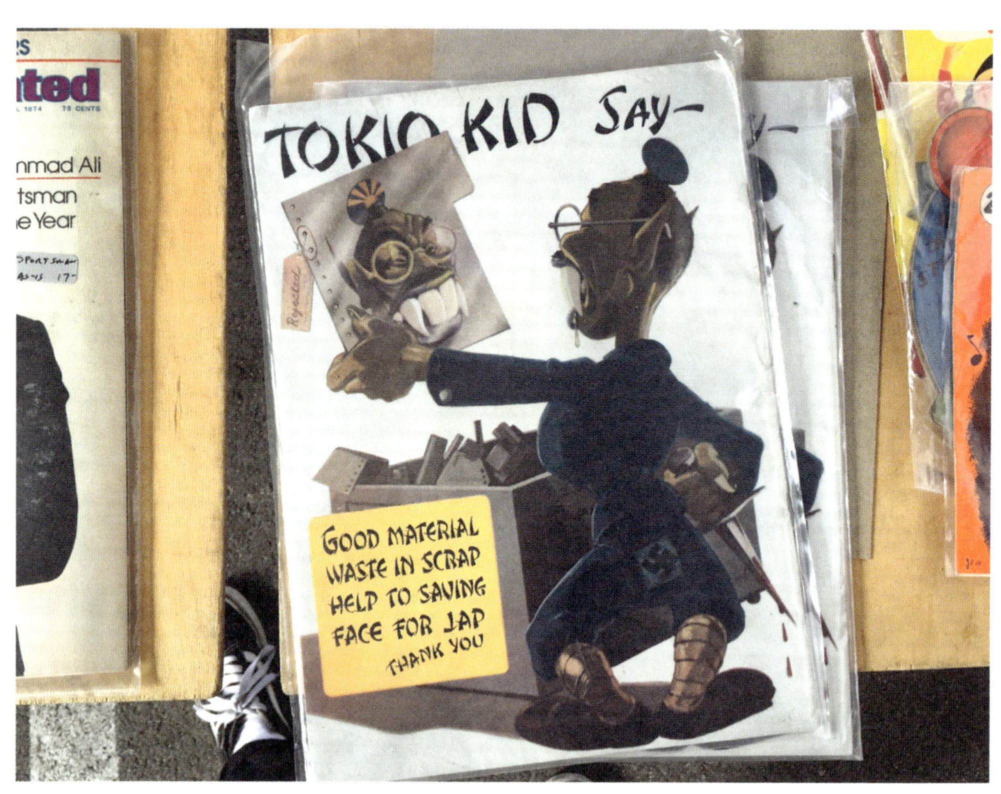
TOKIO KID Say—
Rejected
GOOD MATERIAL
WASTE IN SCRAP
HELP TO SAVING
FACE FOR JAP
THANK YOU

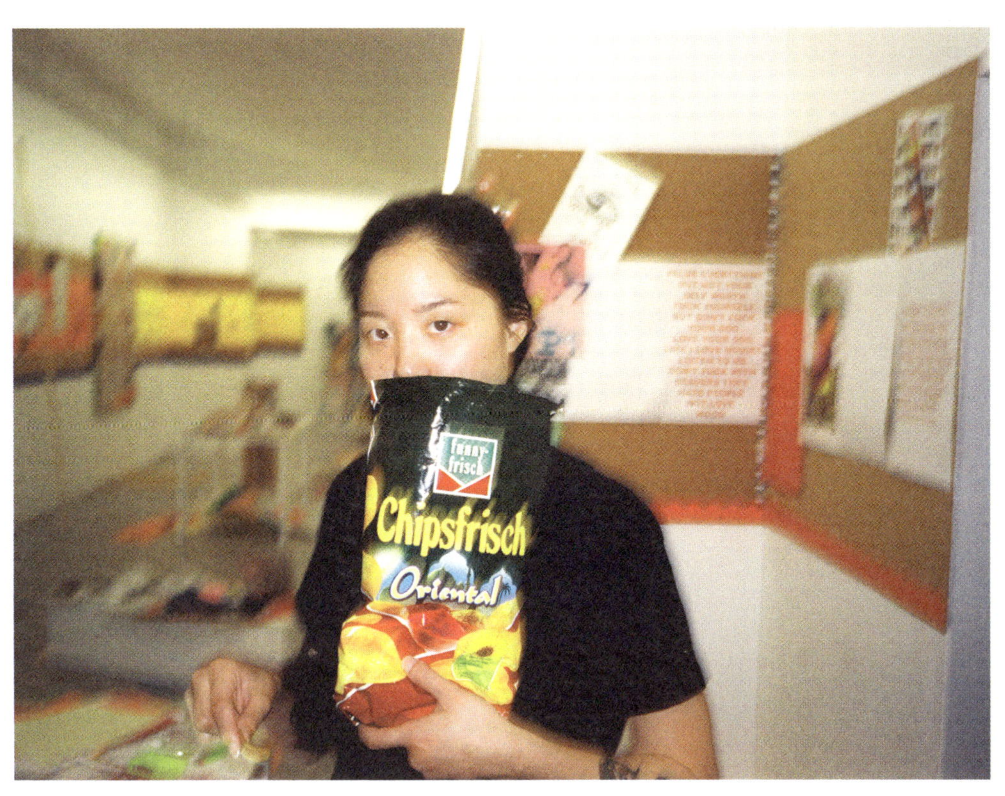
funny-frisch
Chipsfrisch
Oriental

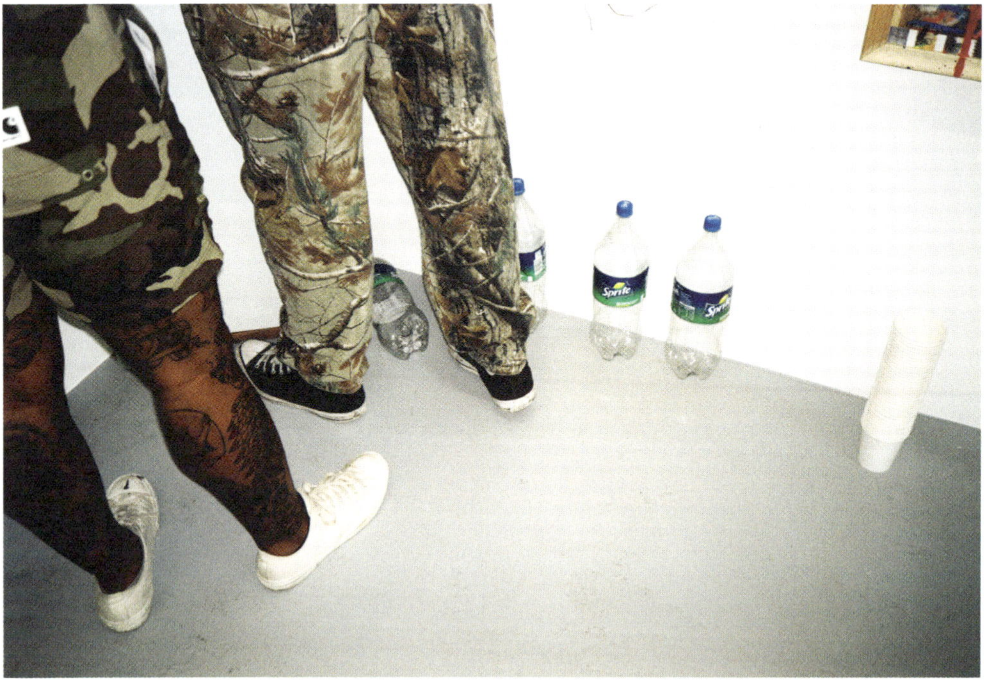

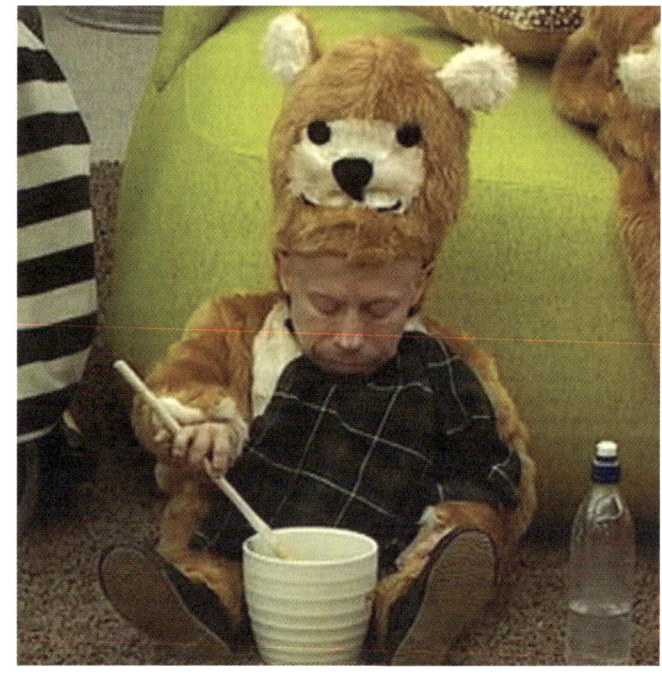

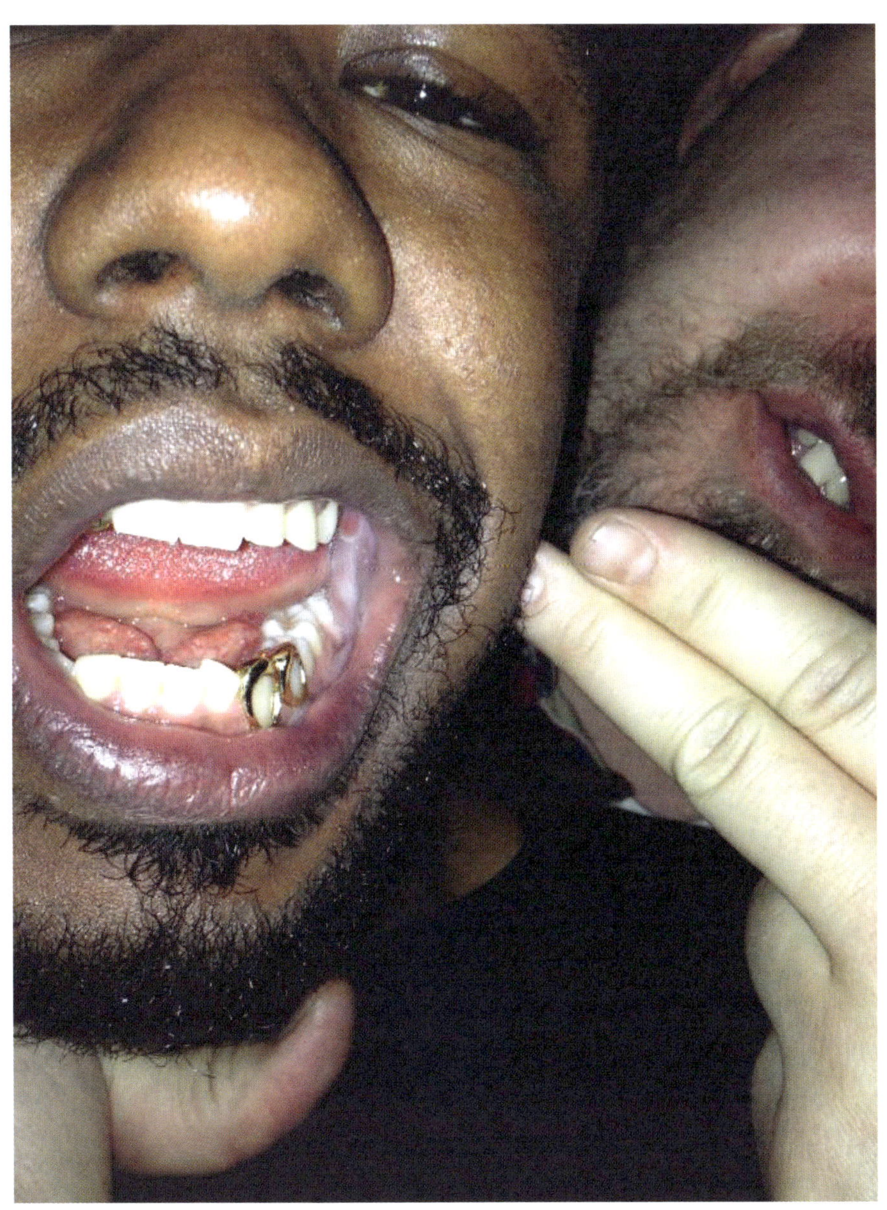

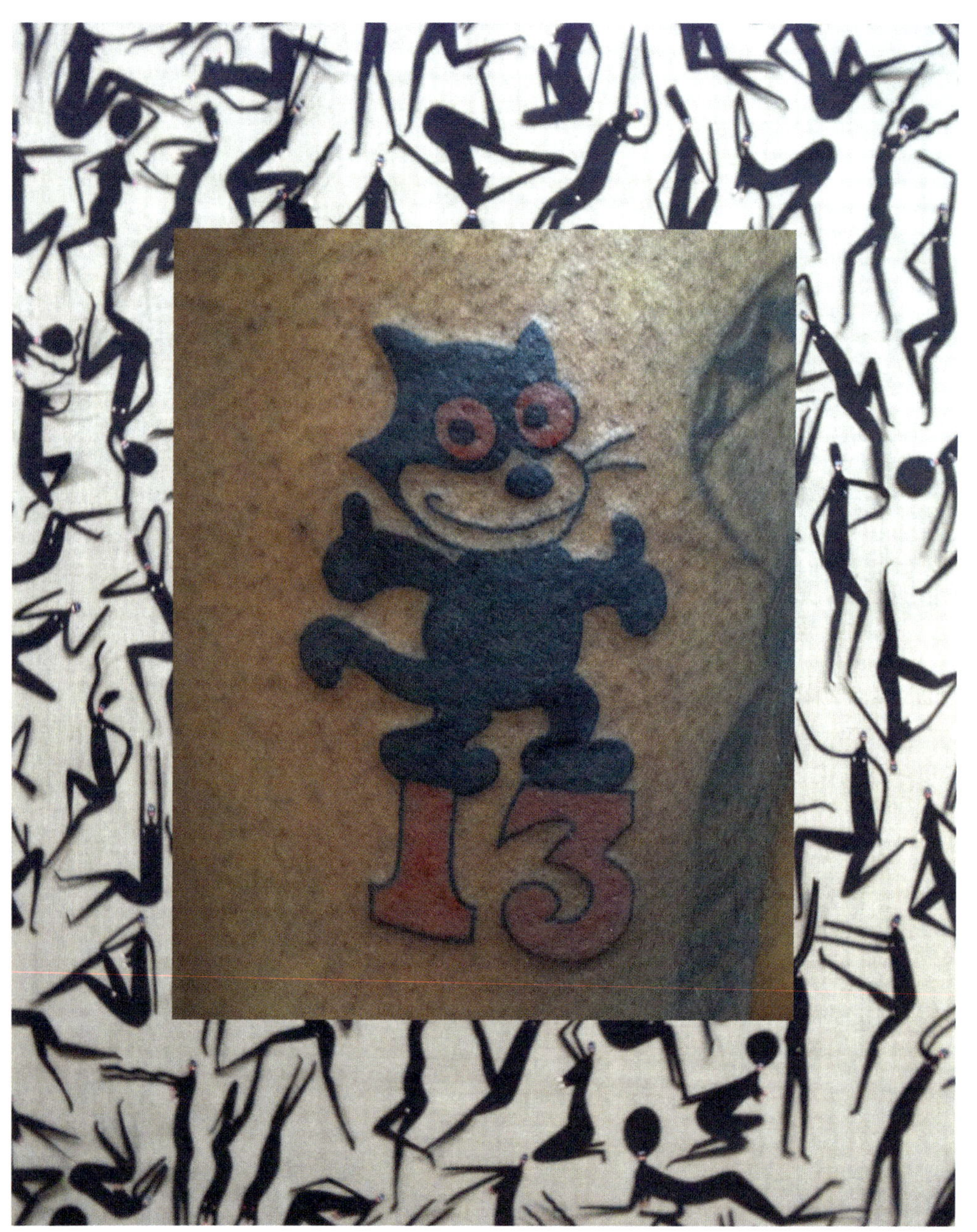
13

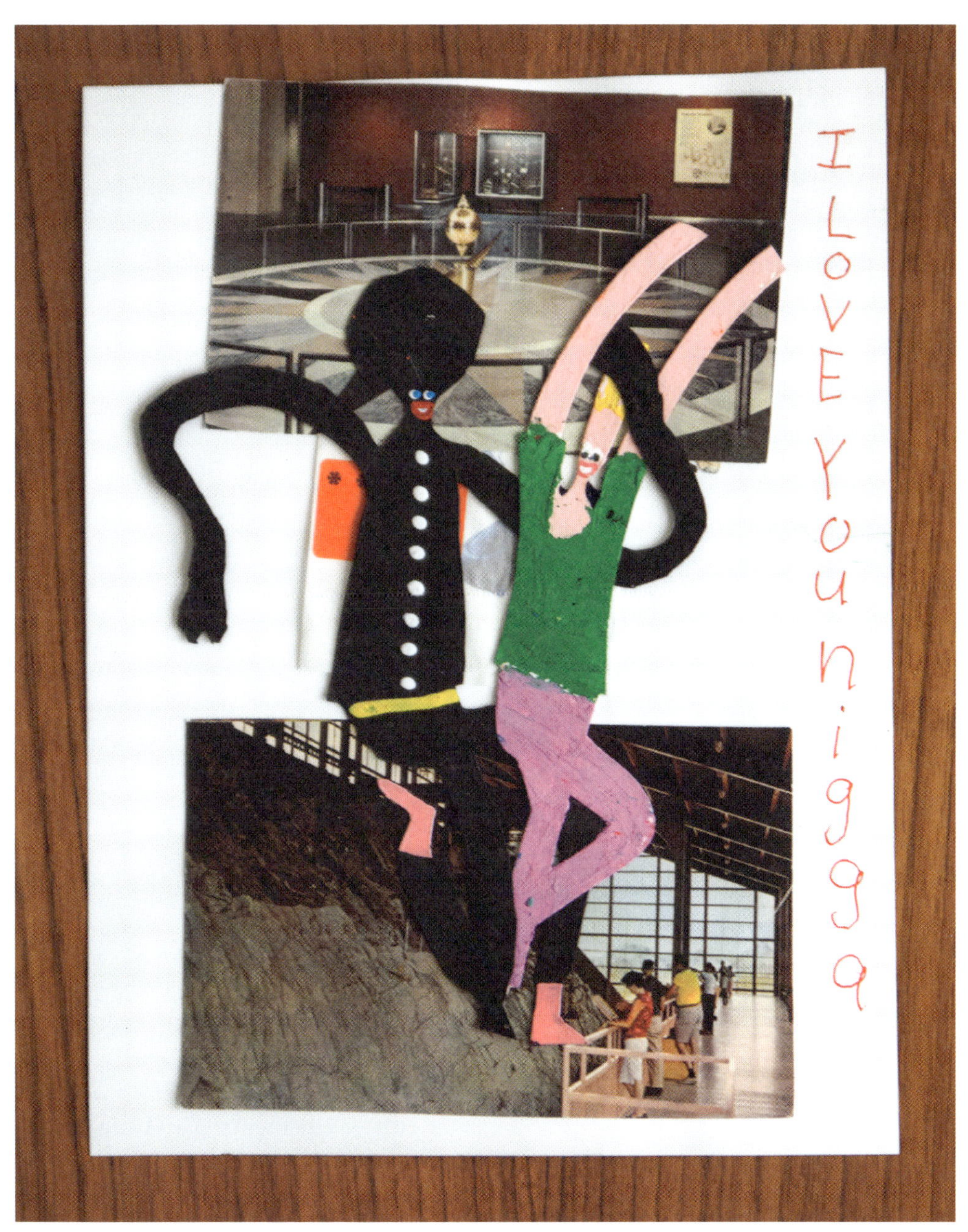
I LOVE YOU nigga

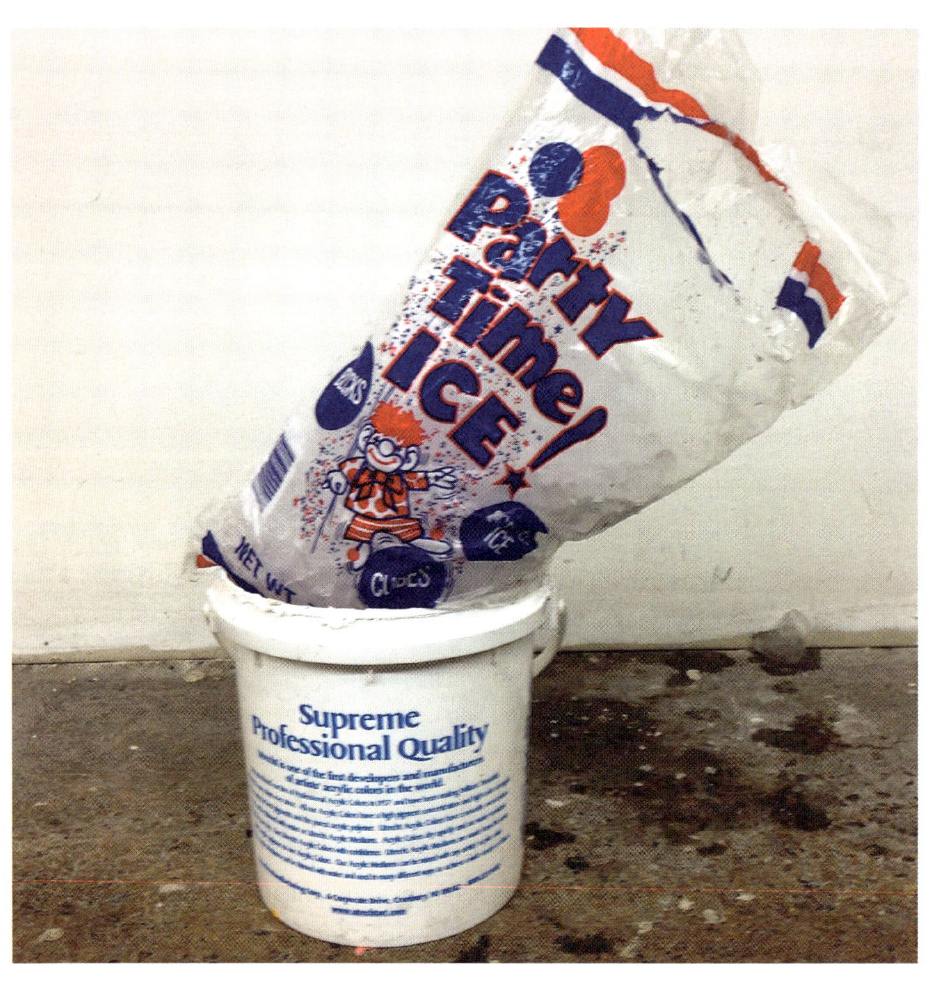

grab the party bag

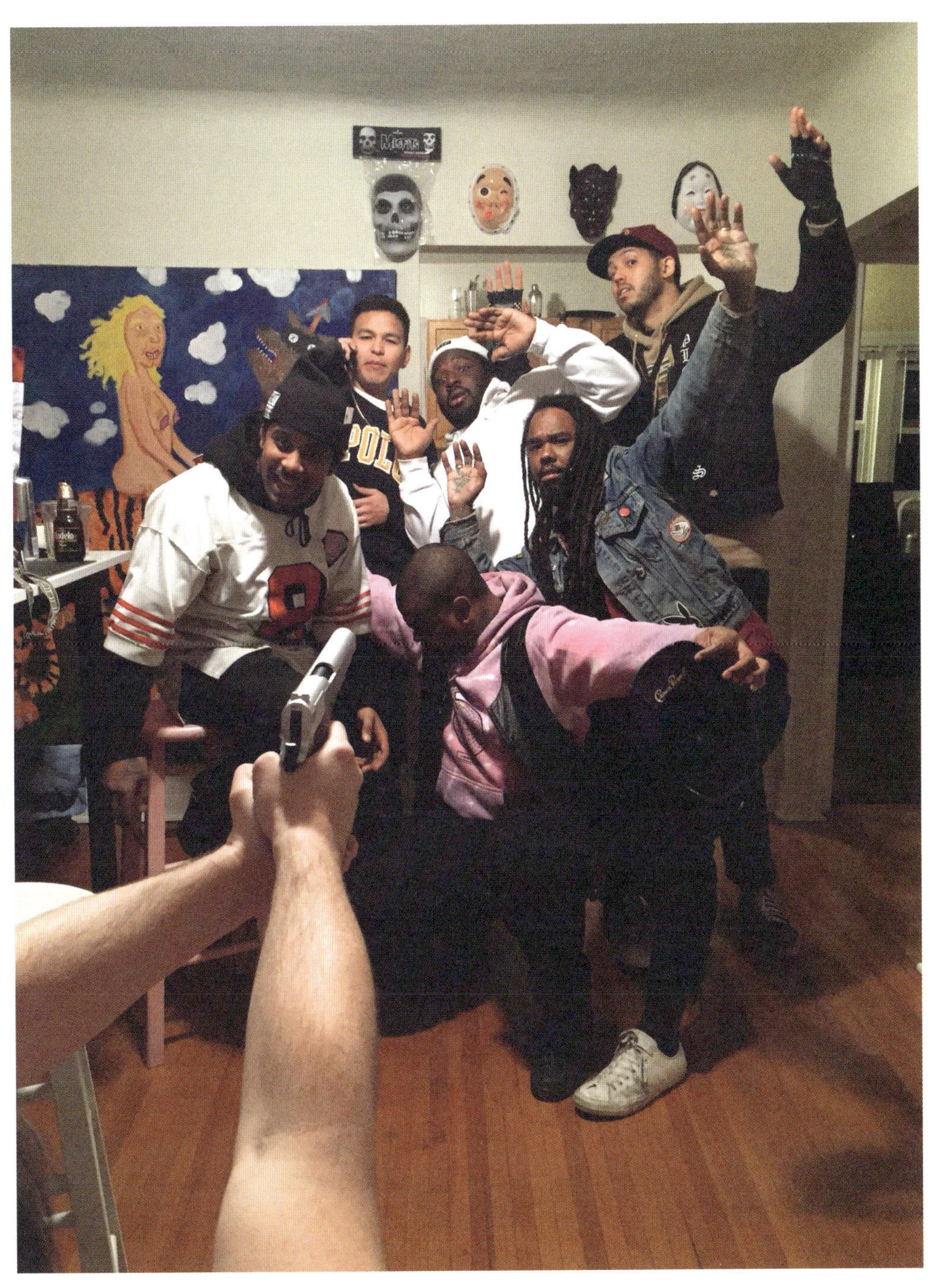

when something goes missing at christmas

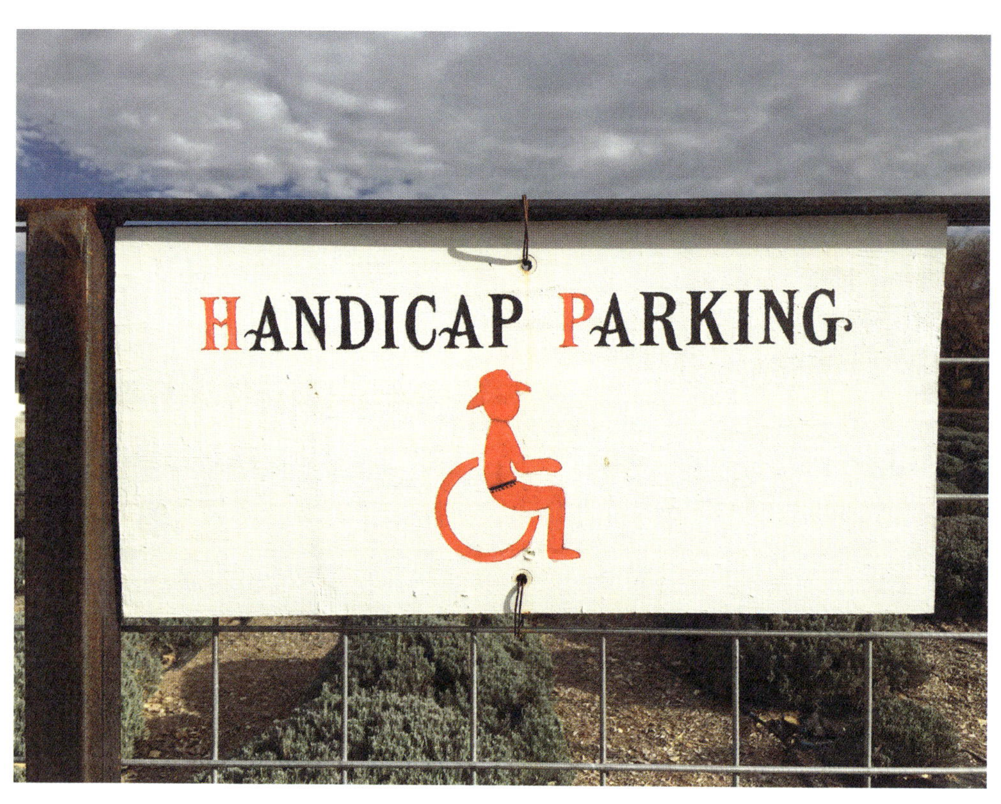
HANDICAP PARKING

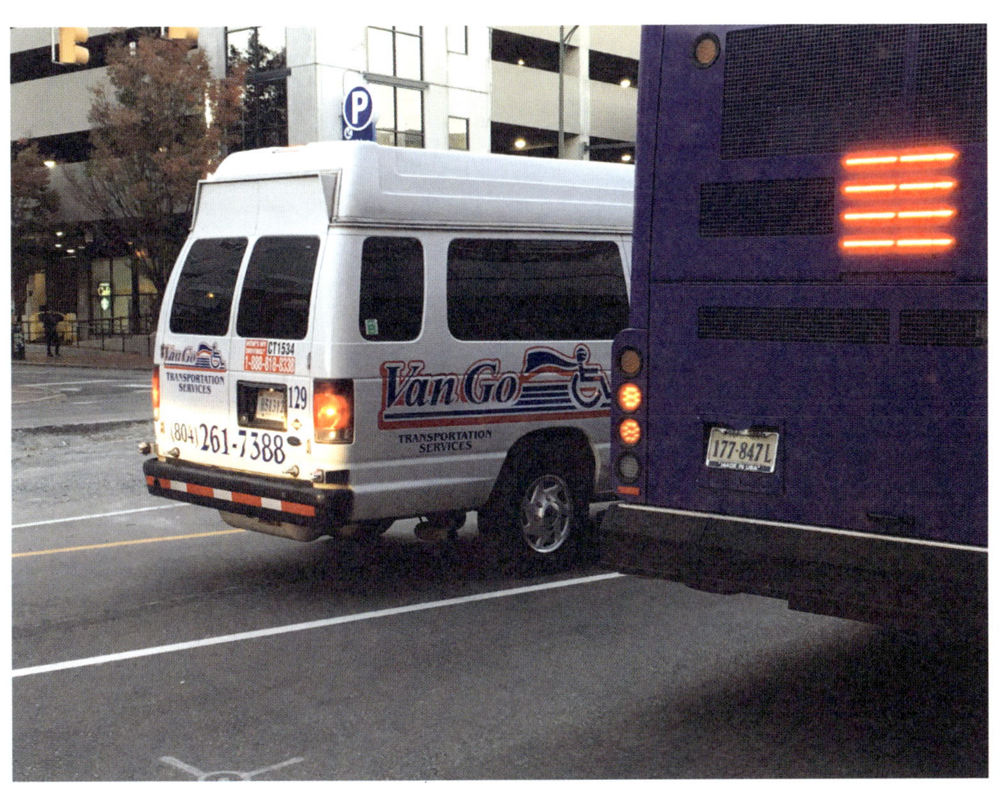

i'd say "protect ya neck," but, you know....

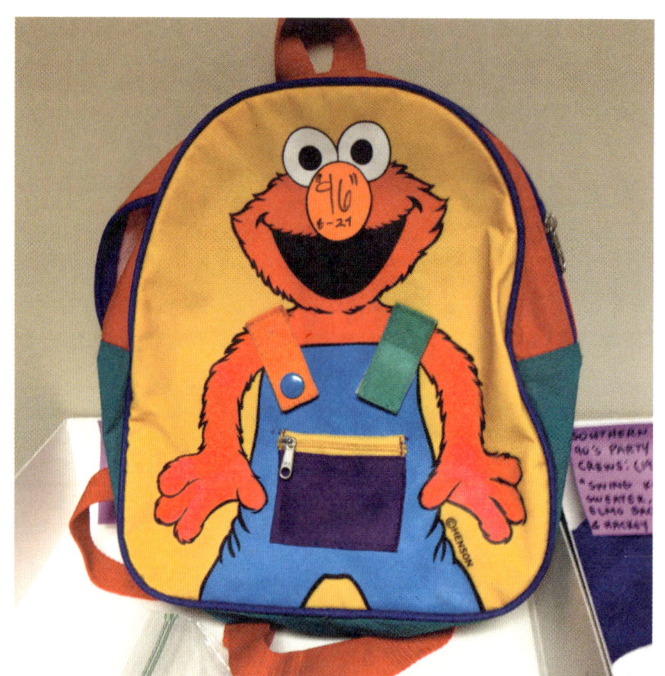

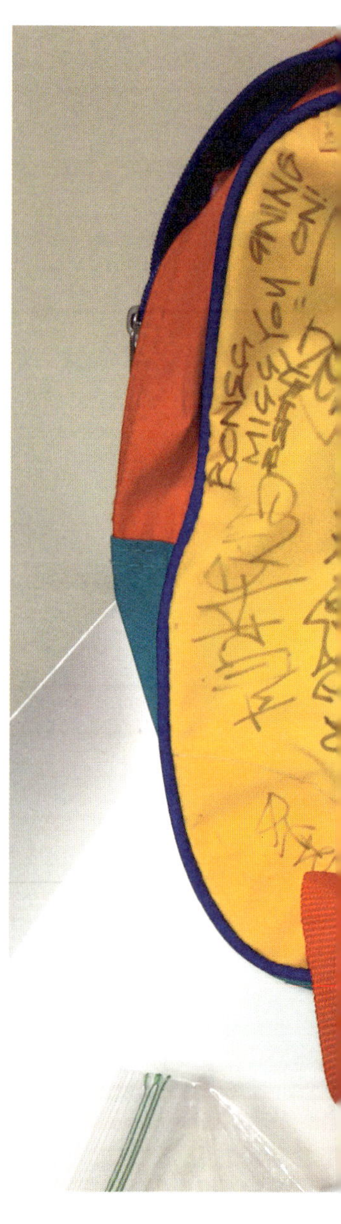

but my cousin told me that southsiders don't play around though

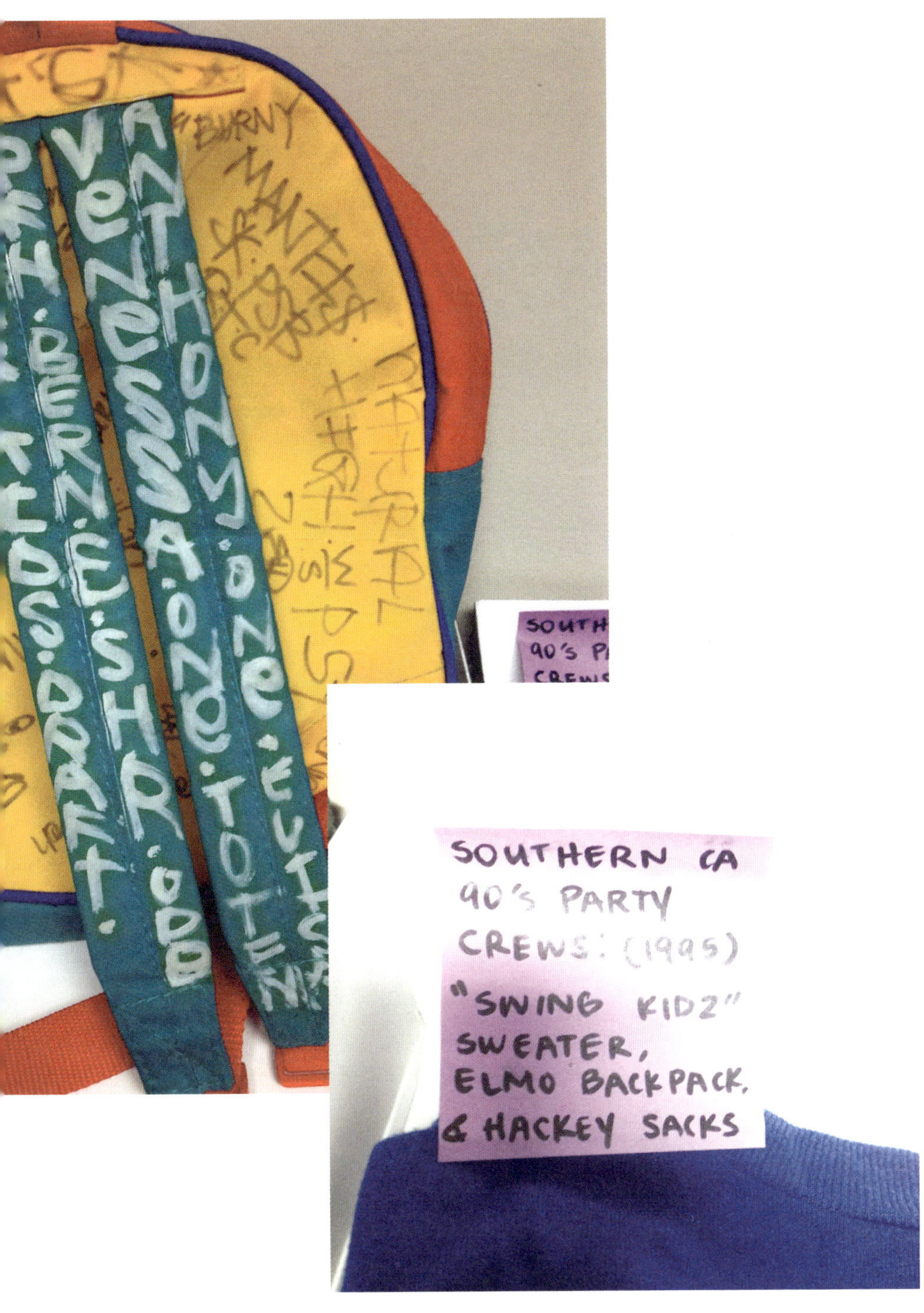
SOUTHERN CA
90's PARTY
CREWS: (1995)
"SWING KIDZ"
SWEATER,
ELMO BACKPACK,
& HACKEY SACKS

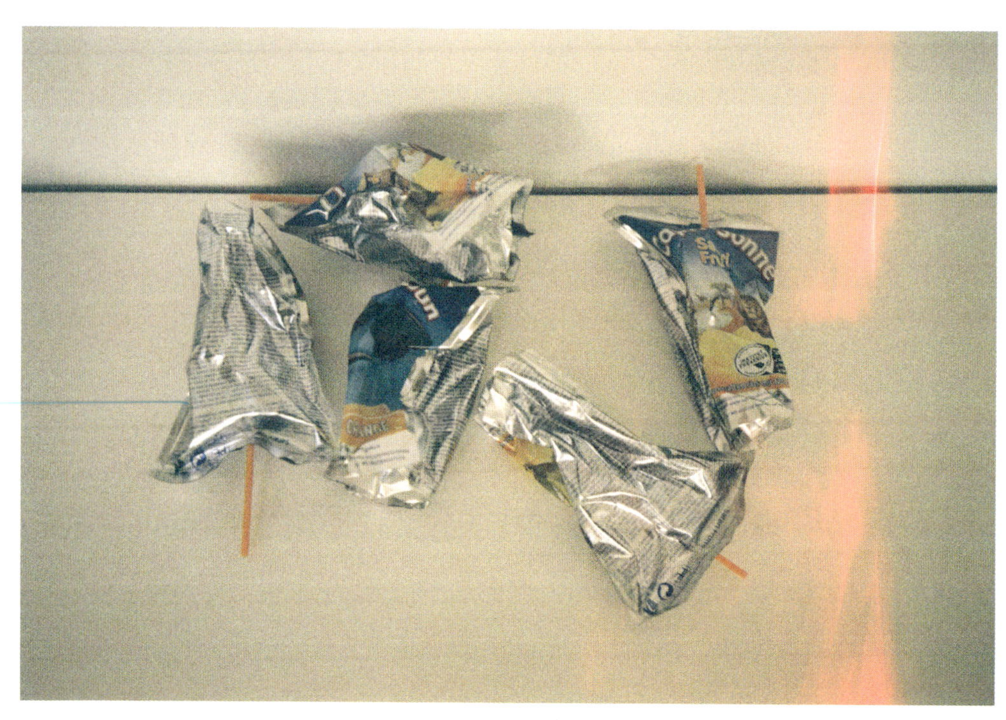

lemme get a pack of slims

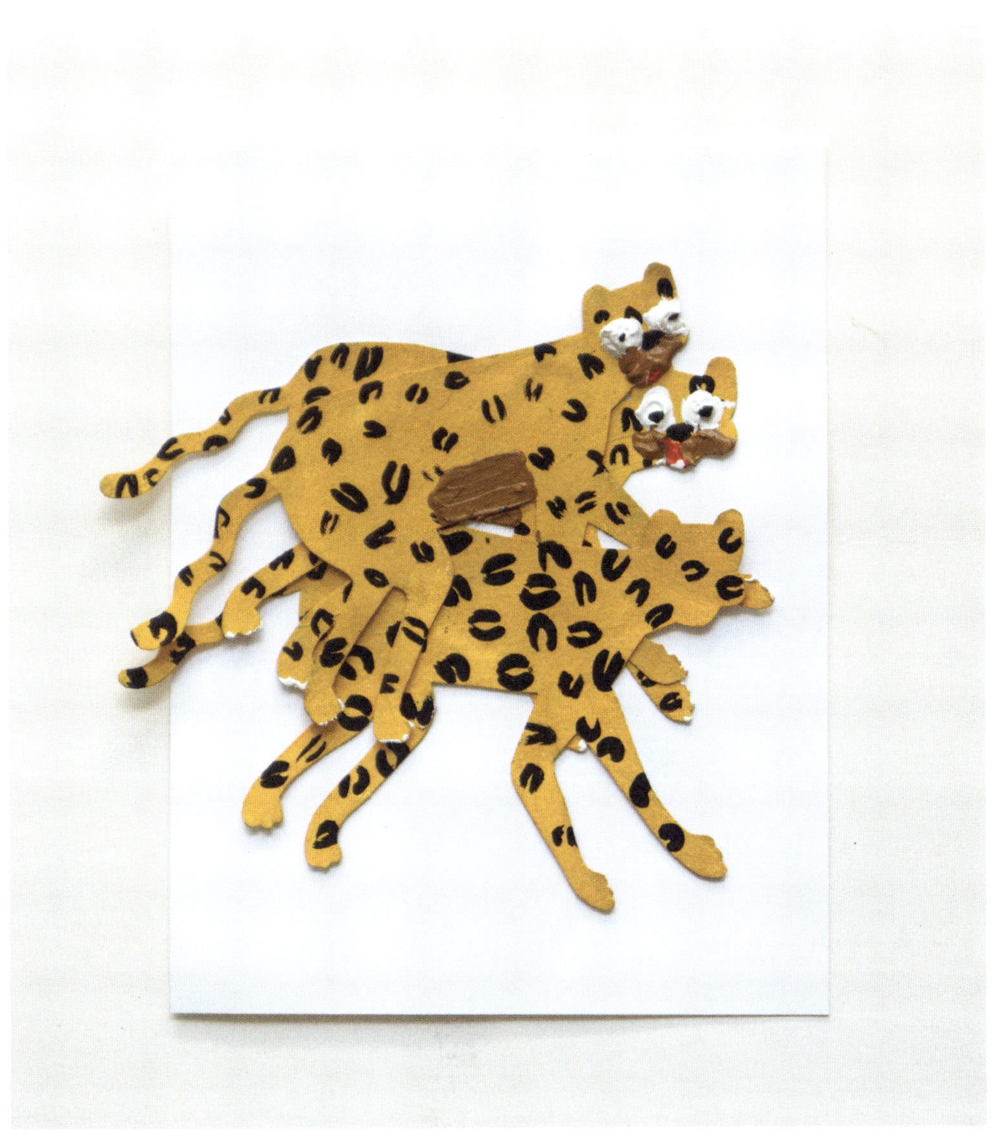

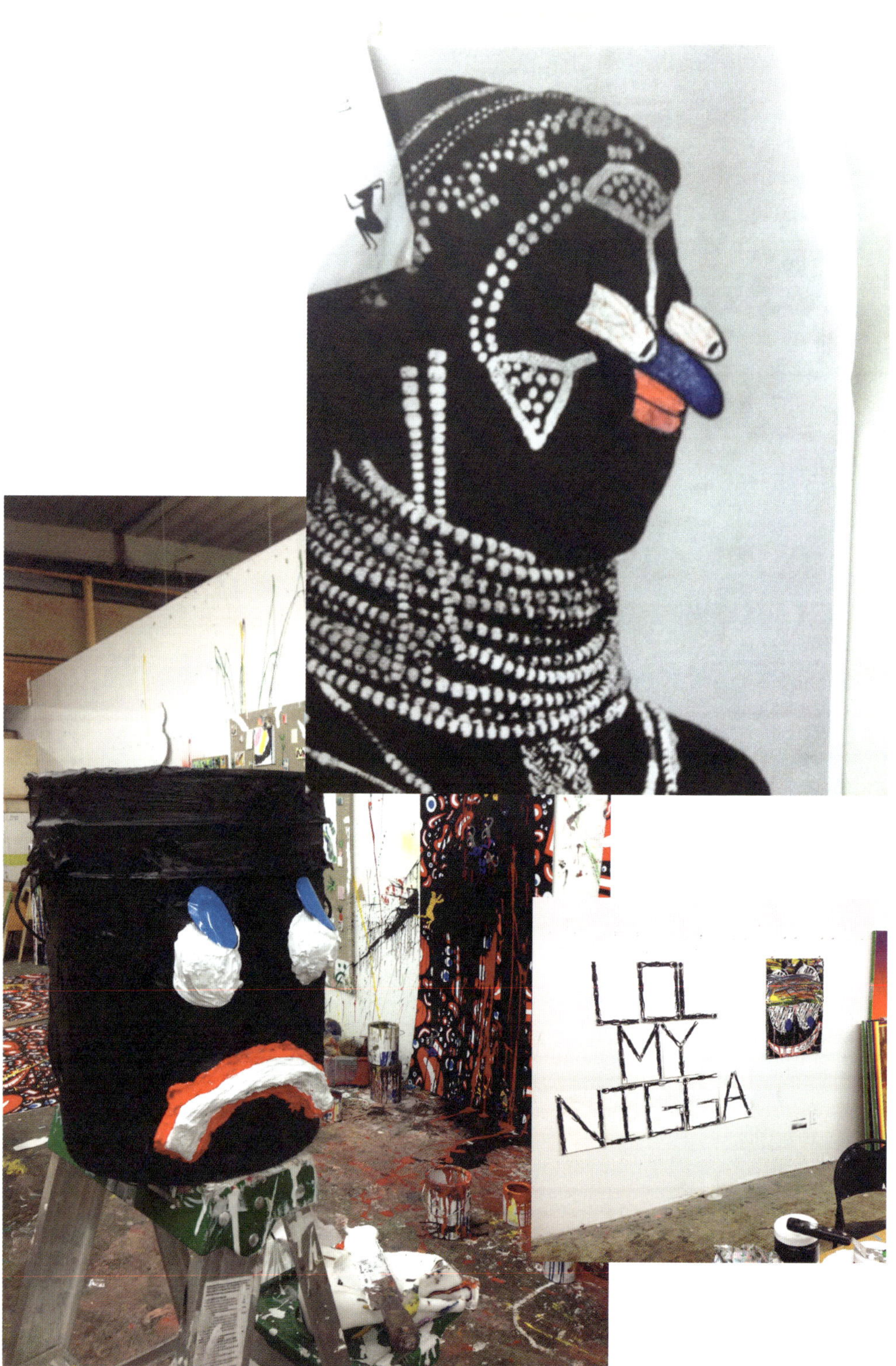
LOL
MY
NIGGA

●●○○○ Verizon 11:35 AM 93%

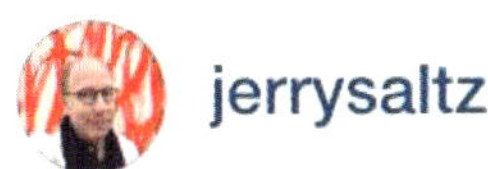

jerrysaltz

4h

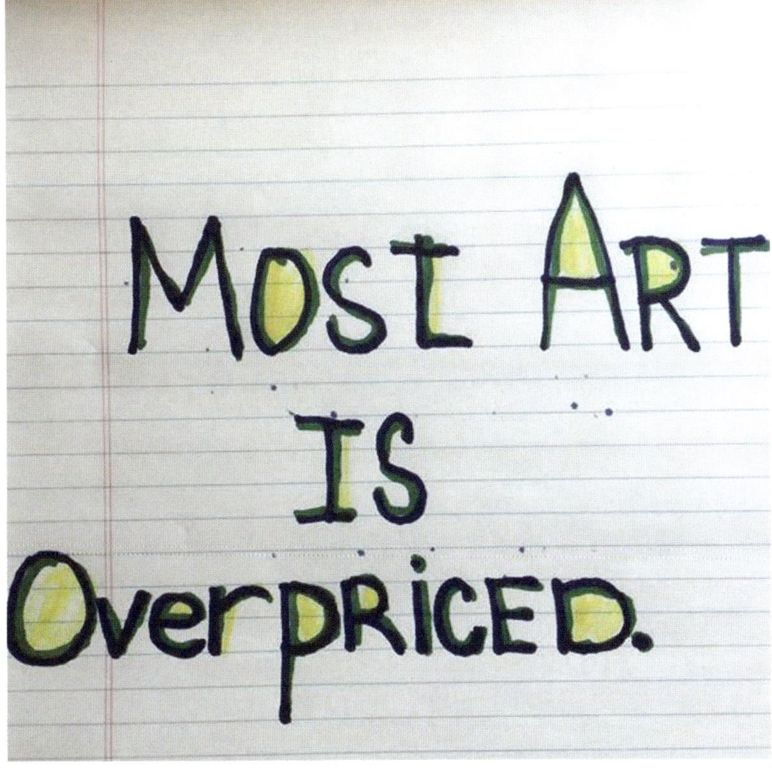

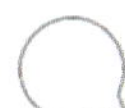 

♥ 4,828 likes

jerrysaltz I know you say "Not my art."

View all 371 comments

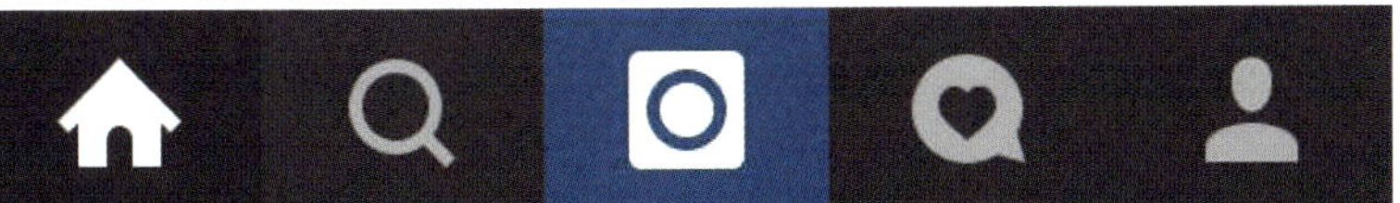

nothing worse than that instagram @fuckjerry

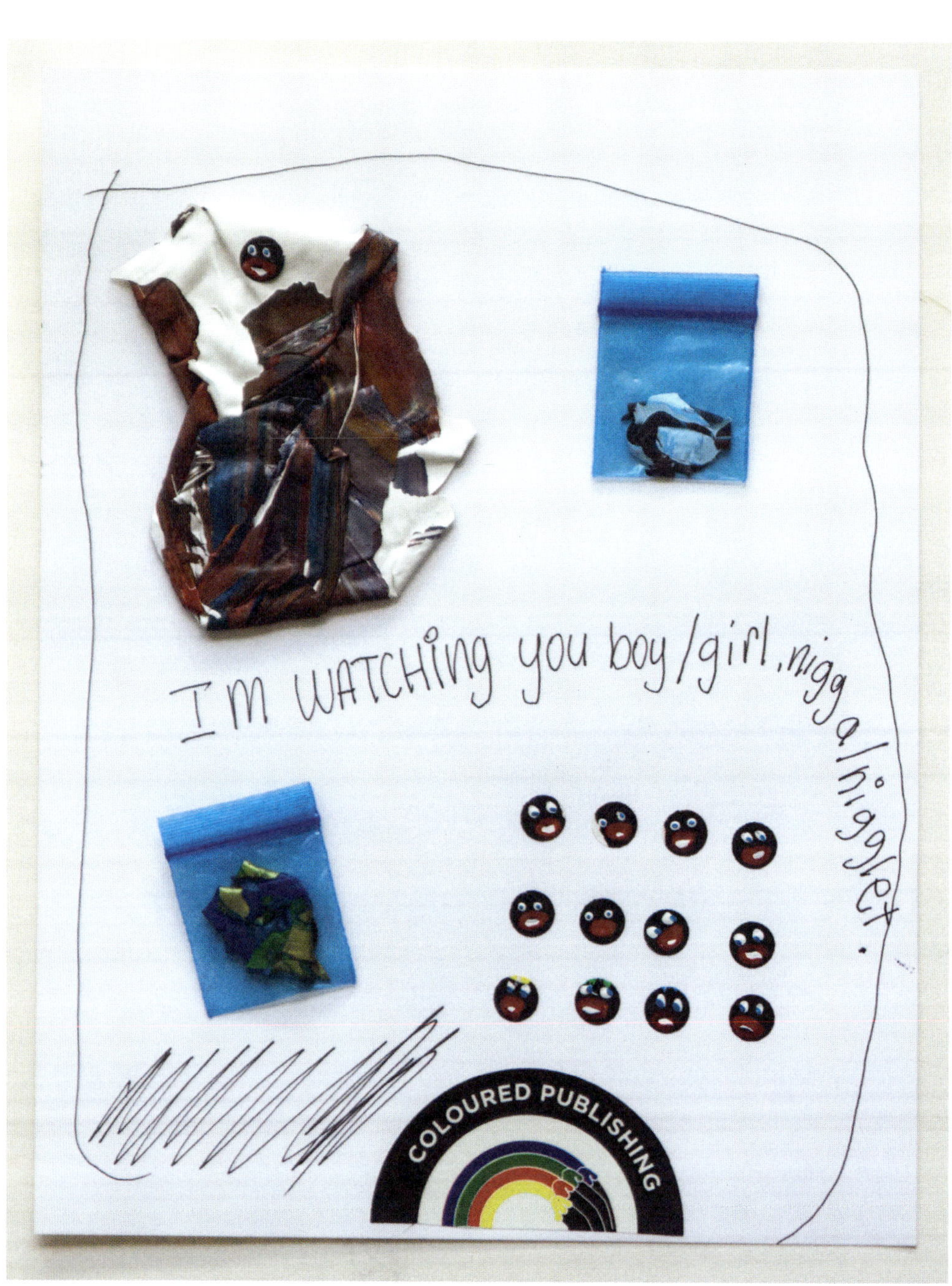
I'M WATCHING you boy/girl, nigga/nigglet.
COLOURED PUBLISHING

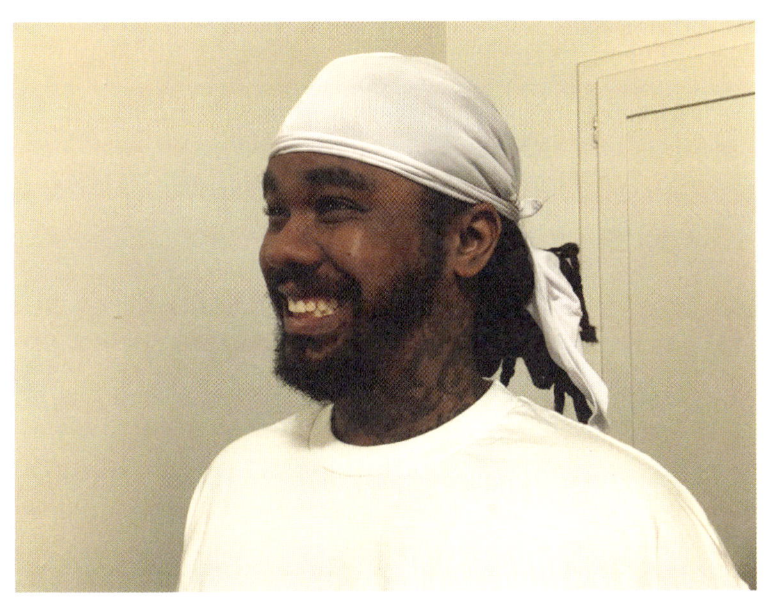

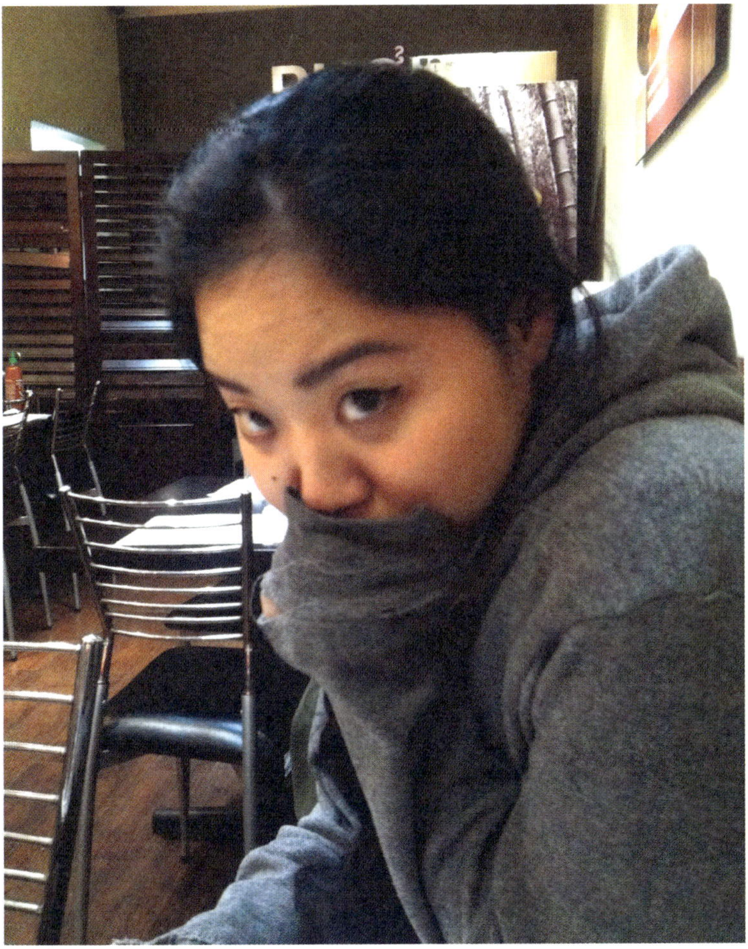

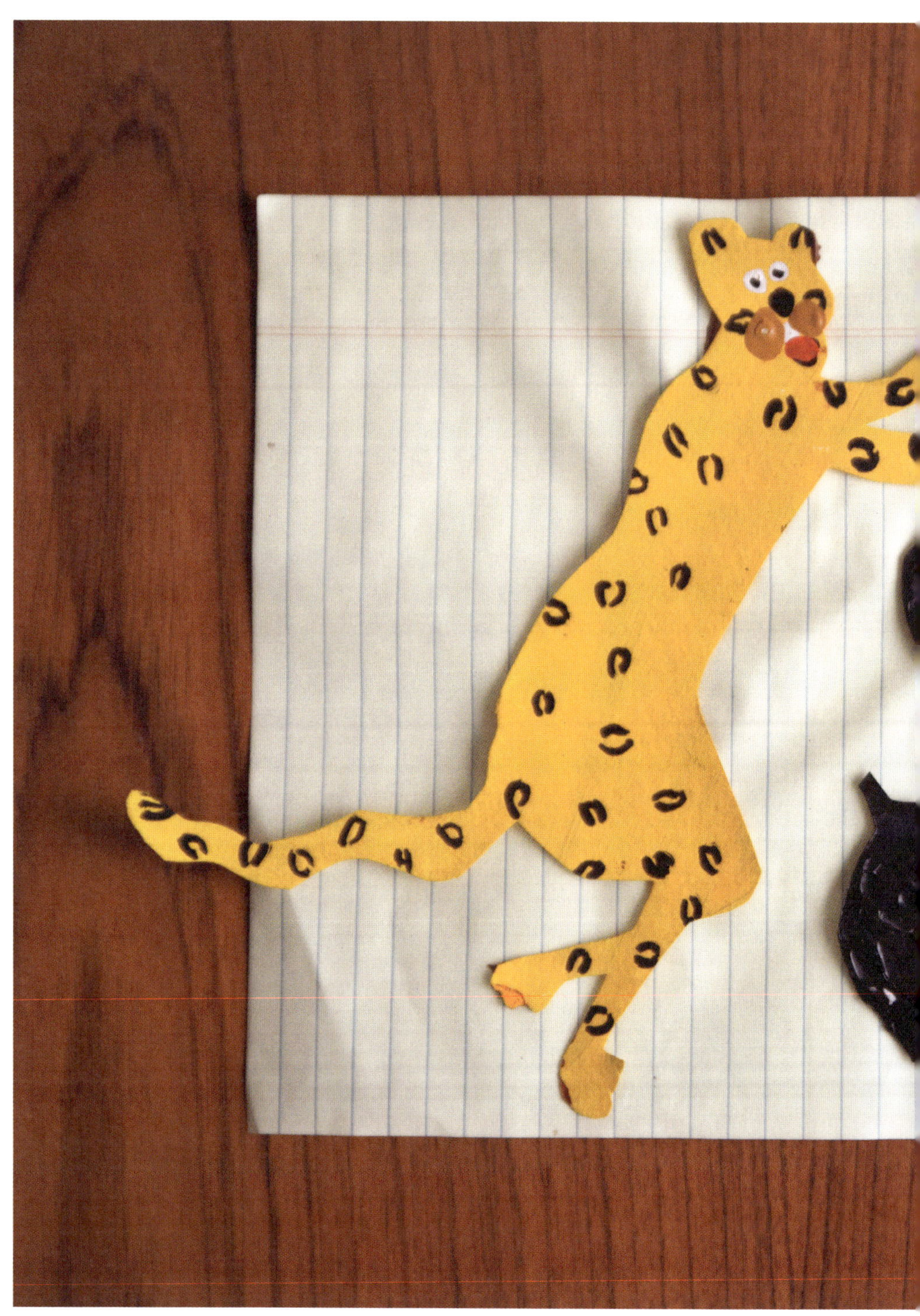

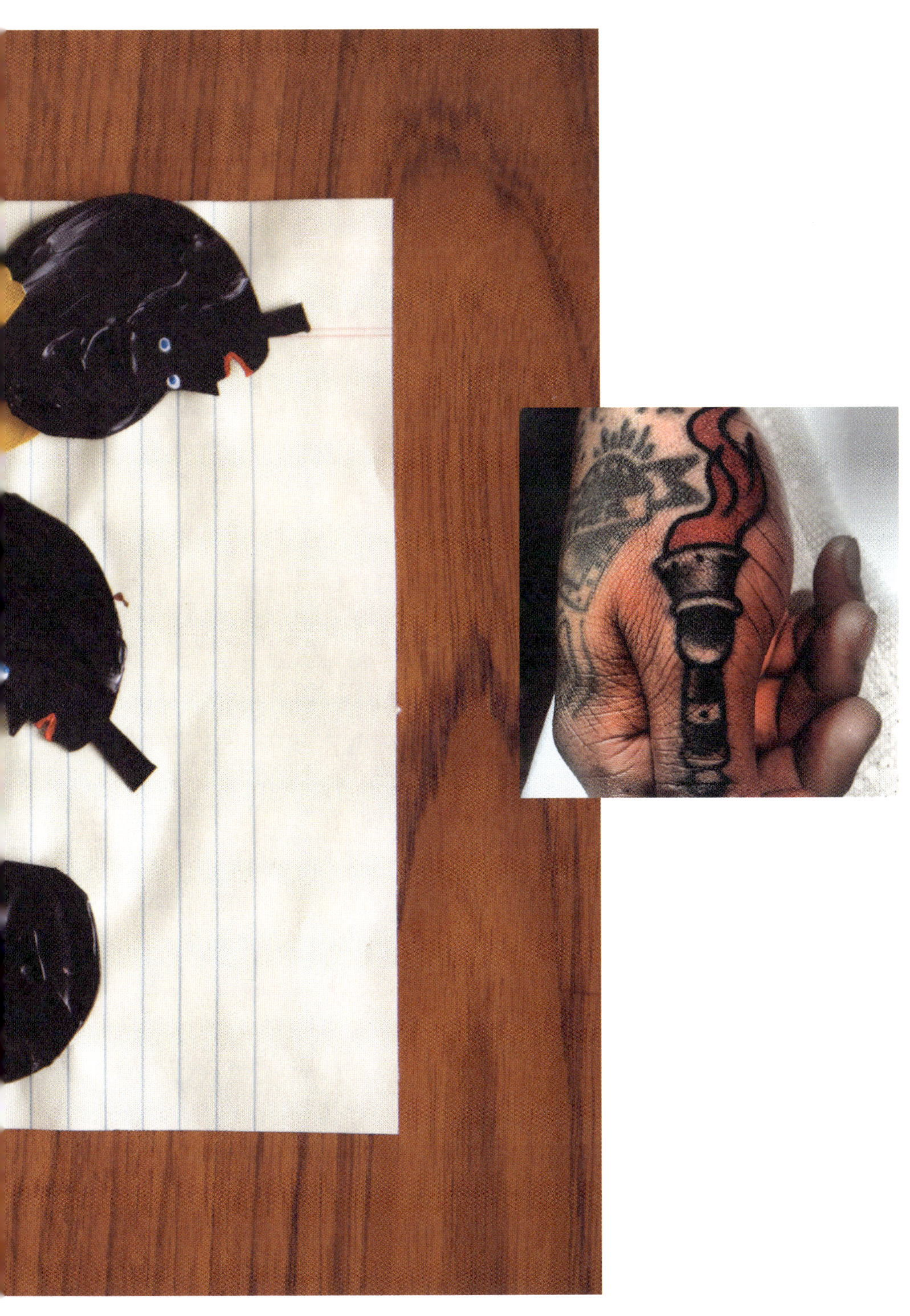

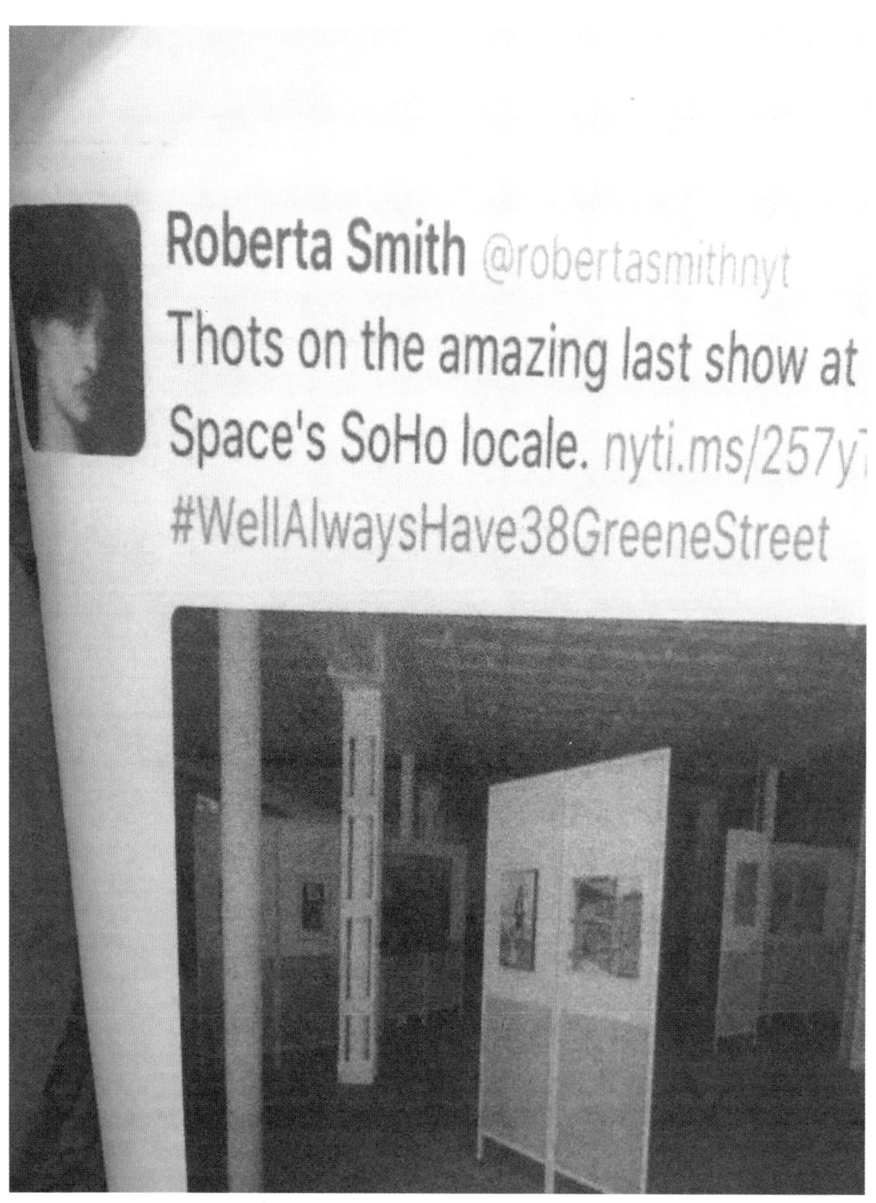
Roberta Smith @robertasmithnyt
Thots on the amazing last show at
Space's SoHo locale. nyti.ms/257y
#WellAlwaysHave38GreeneStreet

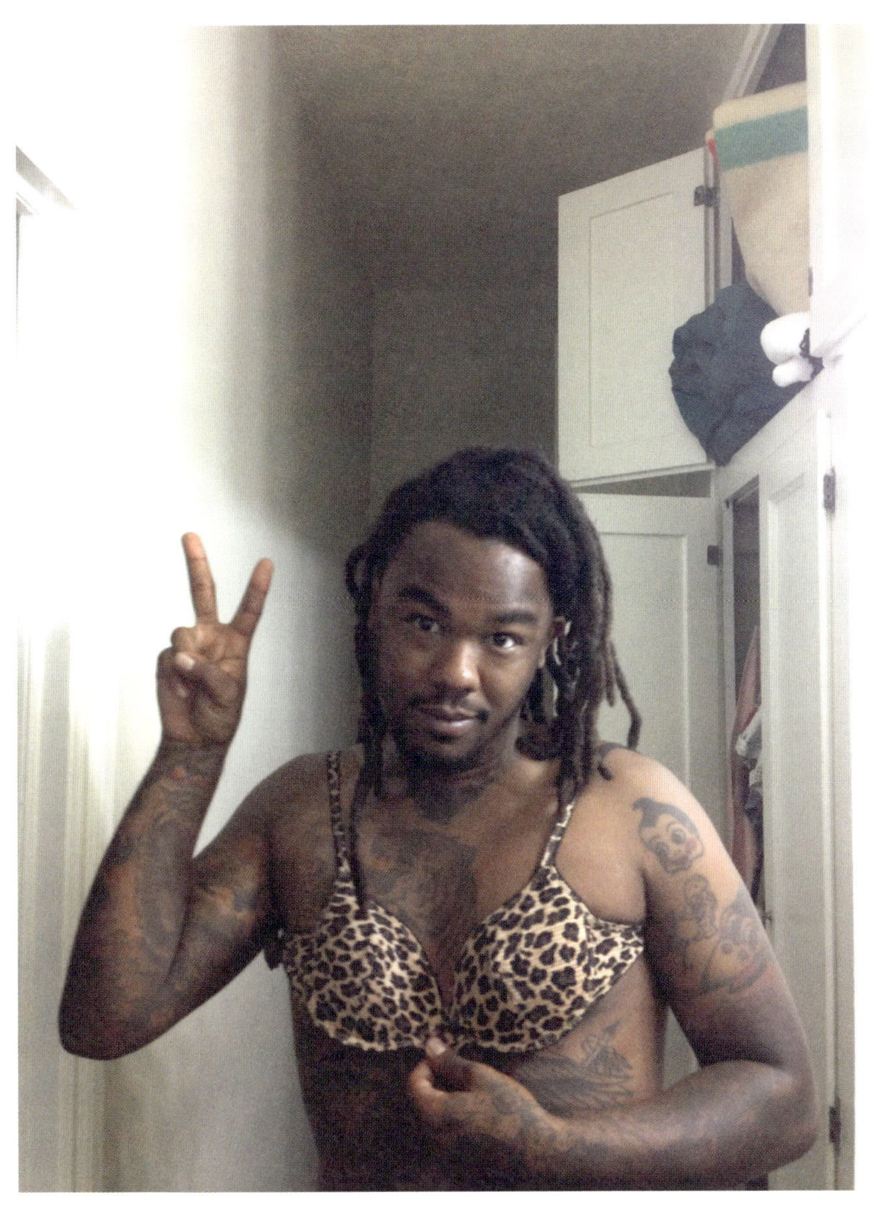

message

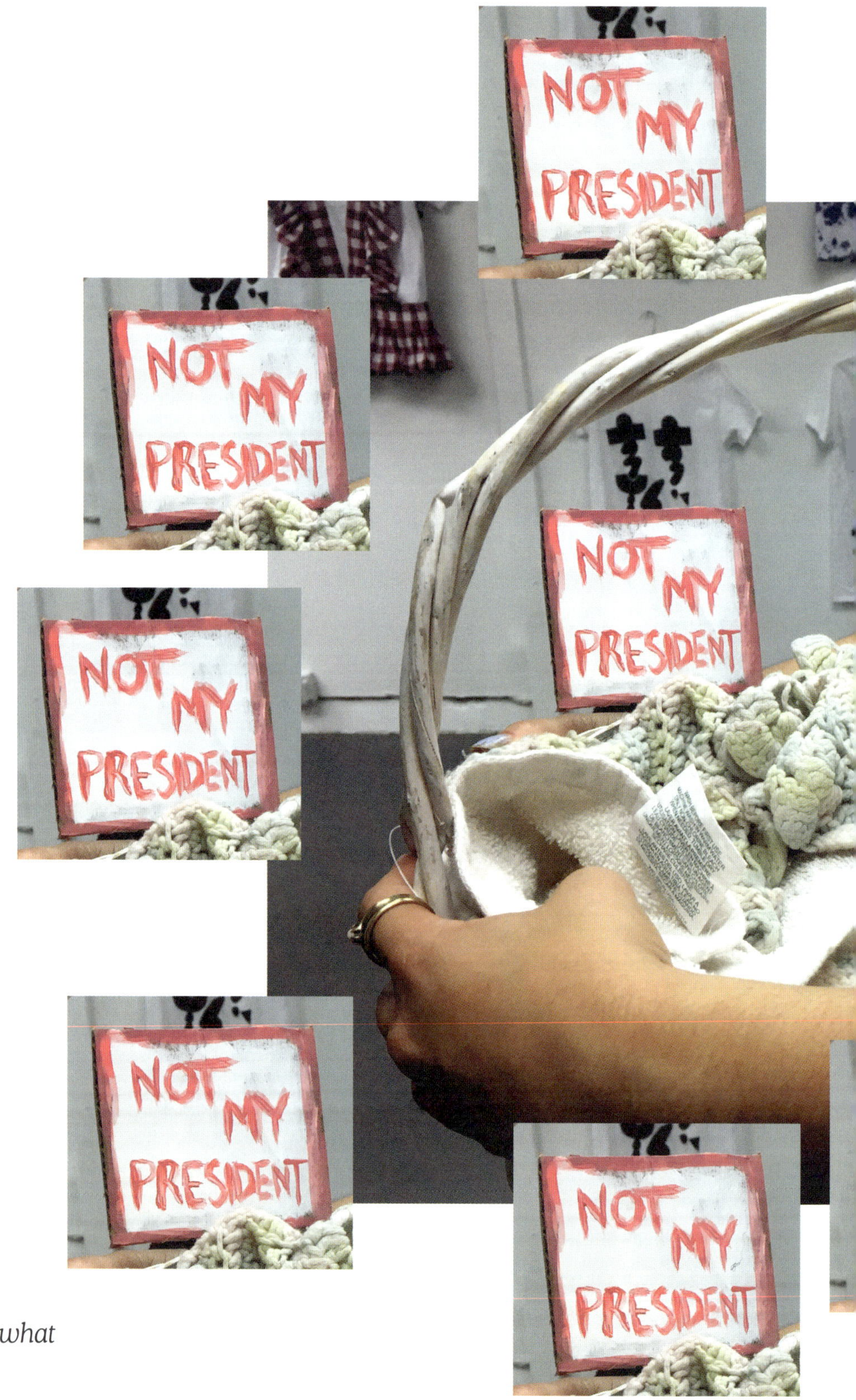

...what

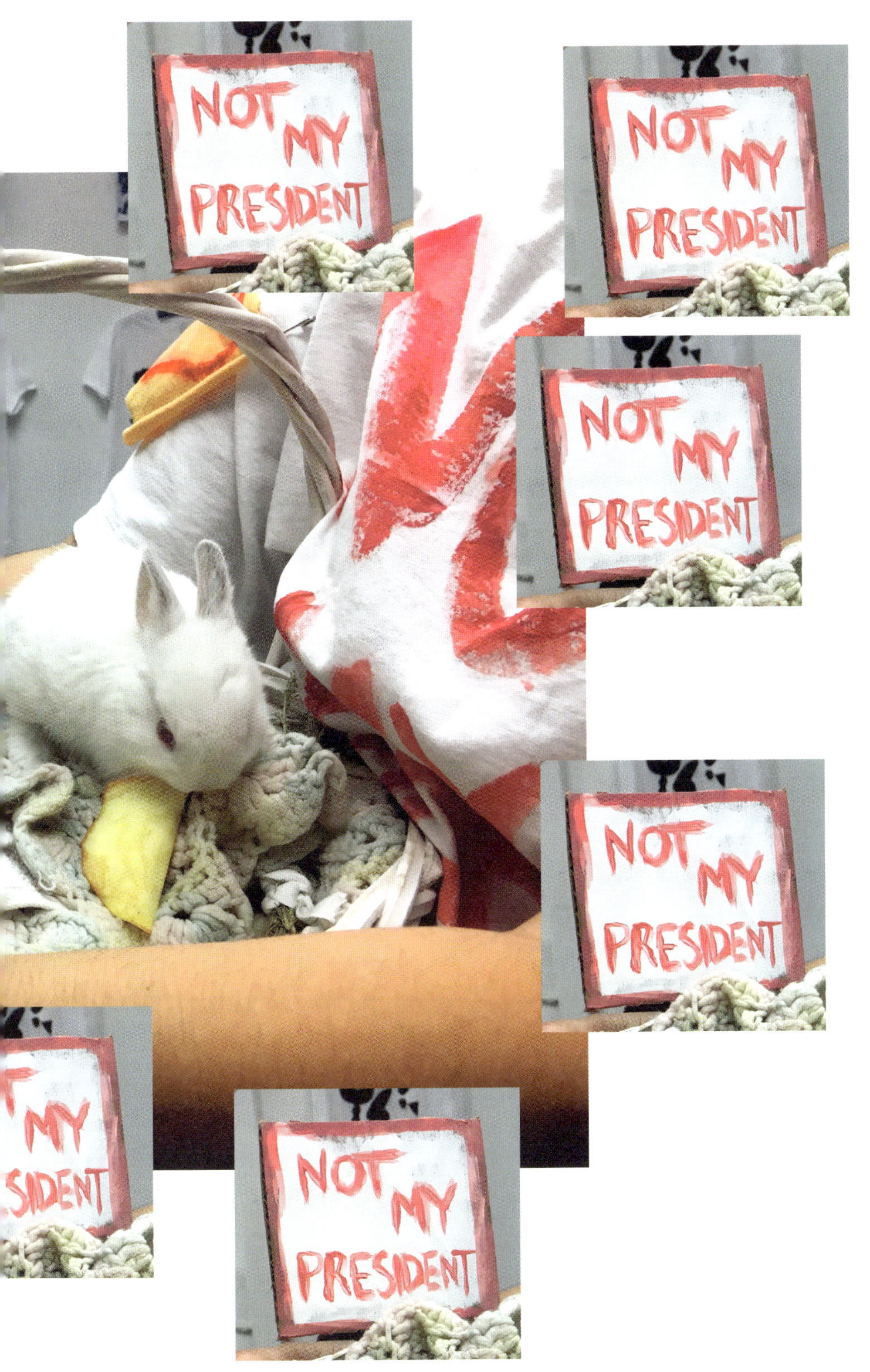
NOT MY PRESIDENT
NOT MY PRESIDENT
NOT MY PRESIDENT
NOT MY PRESIDENT
MY
NOT MY PRESIDENT

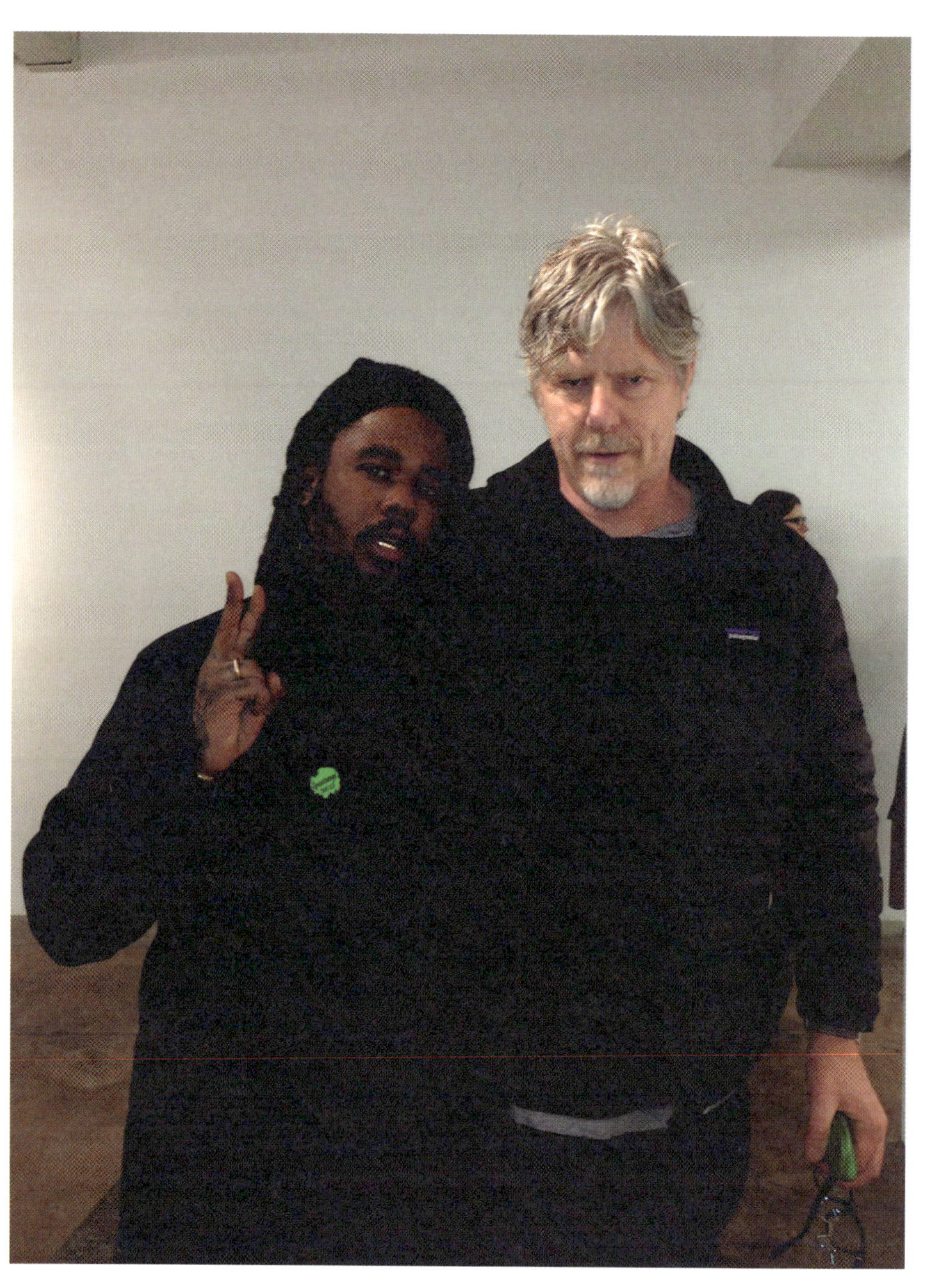

devin and mark grotjahn at moca

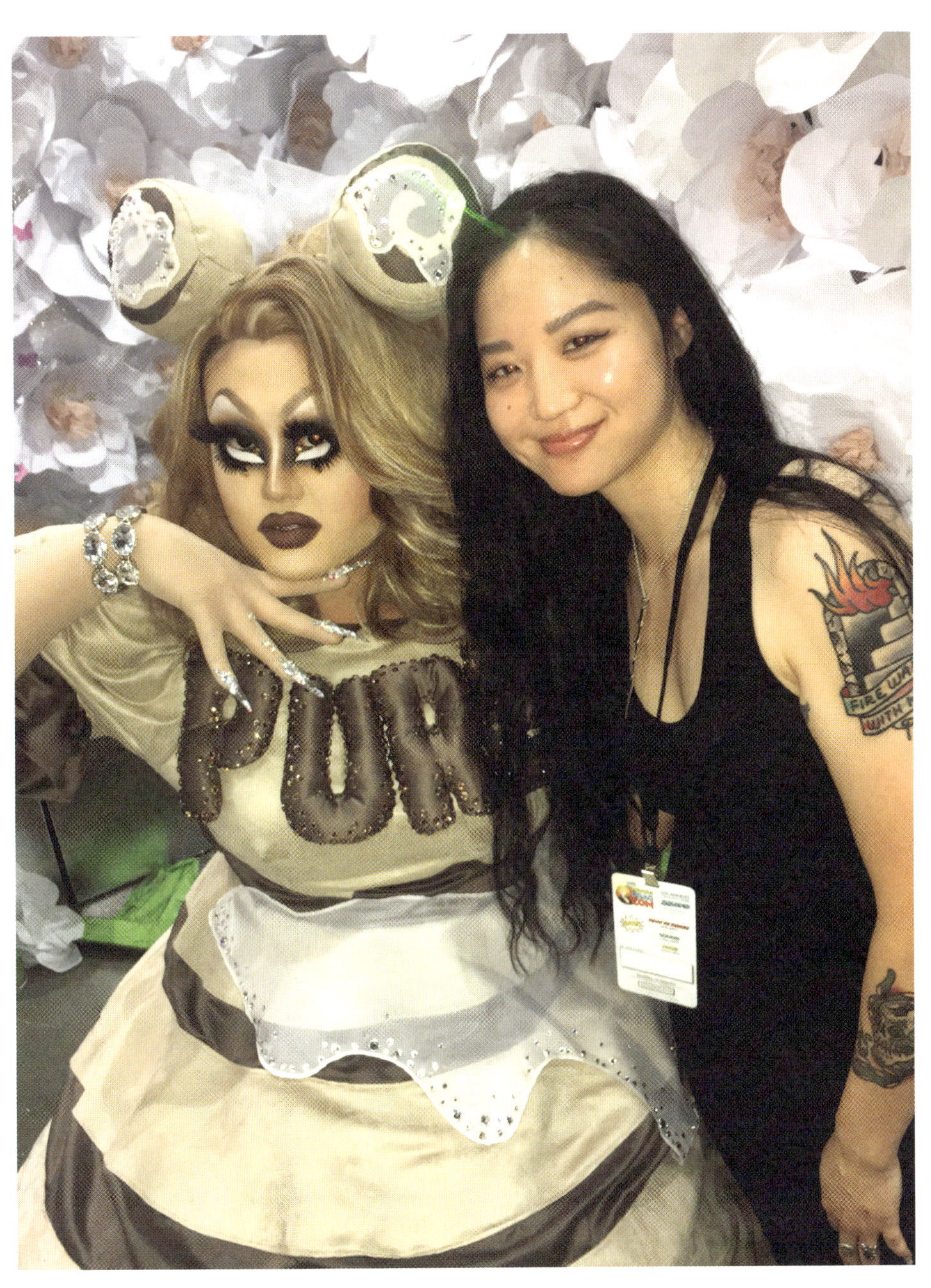

yuri and kim chi at dragcon

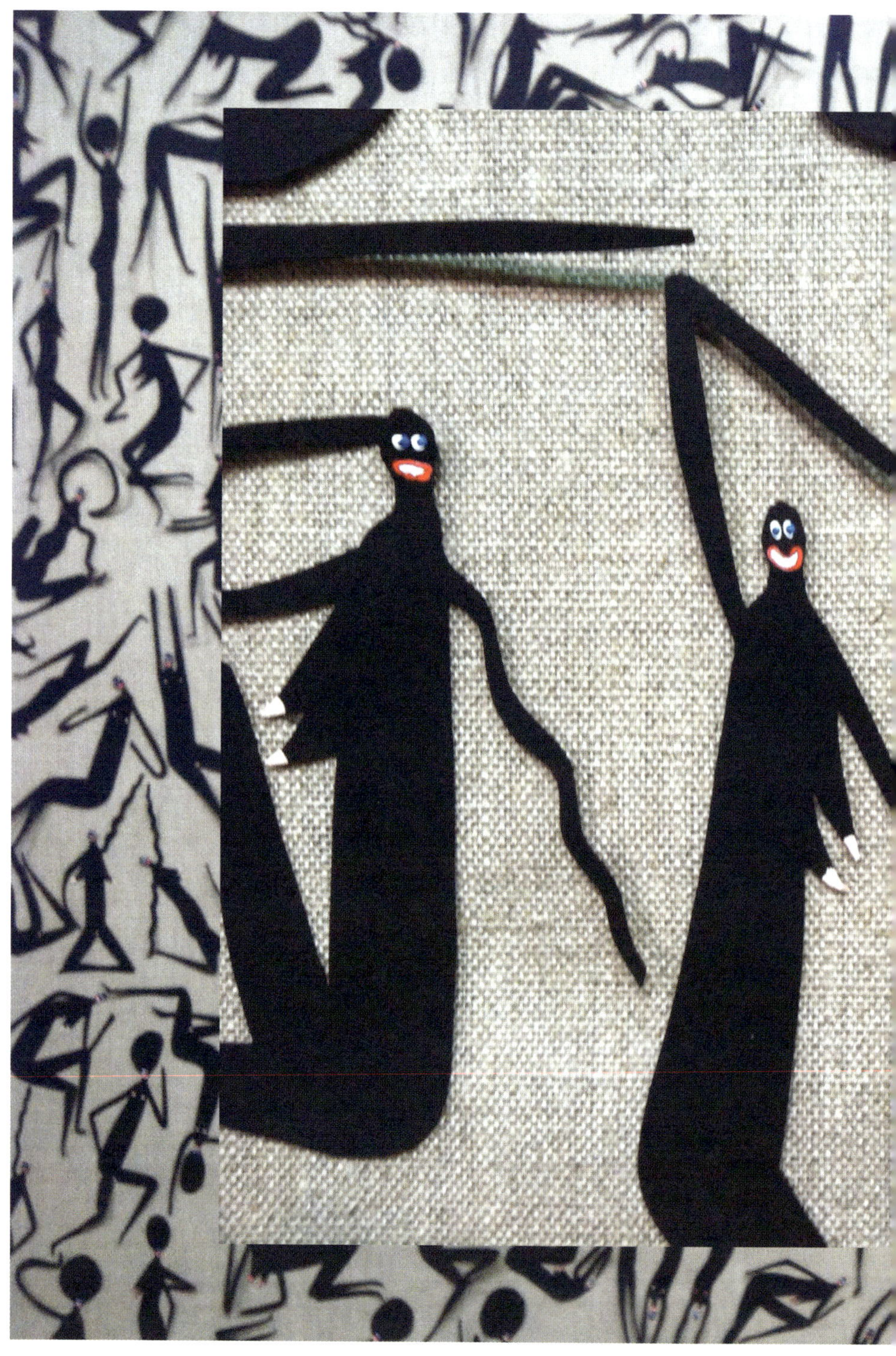

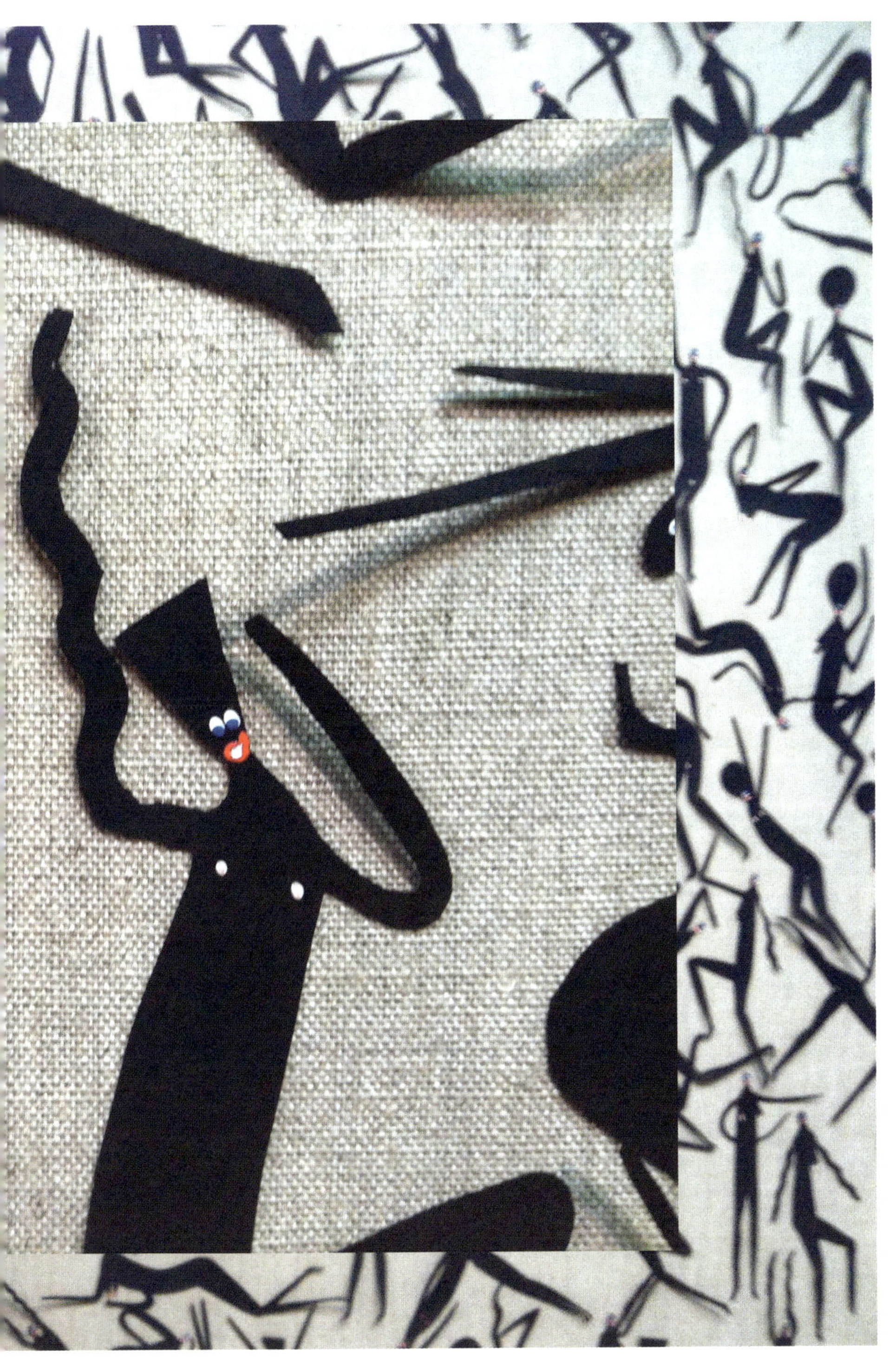

i think that painting is called "297 niggas on linen"

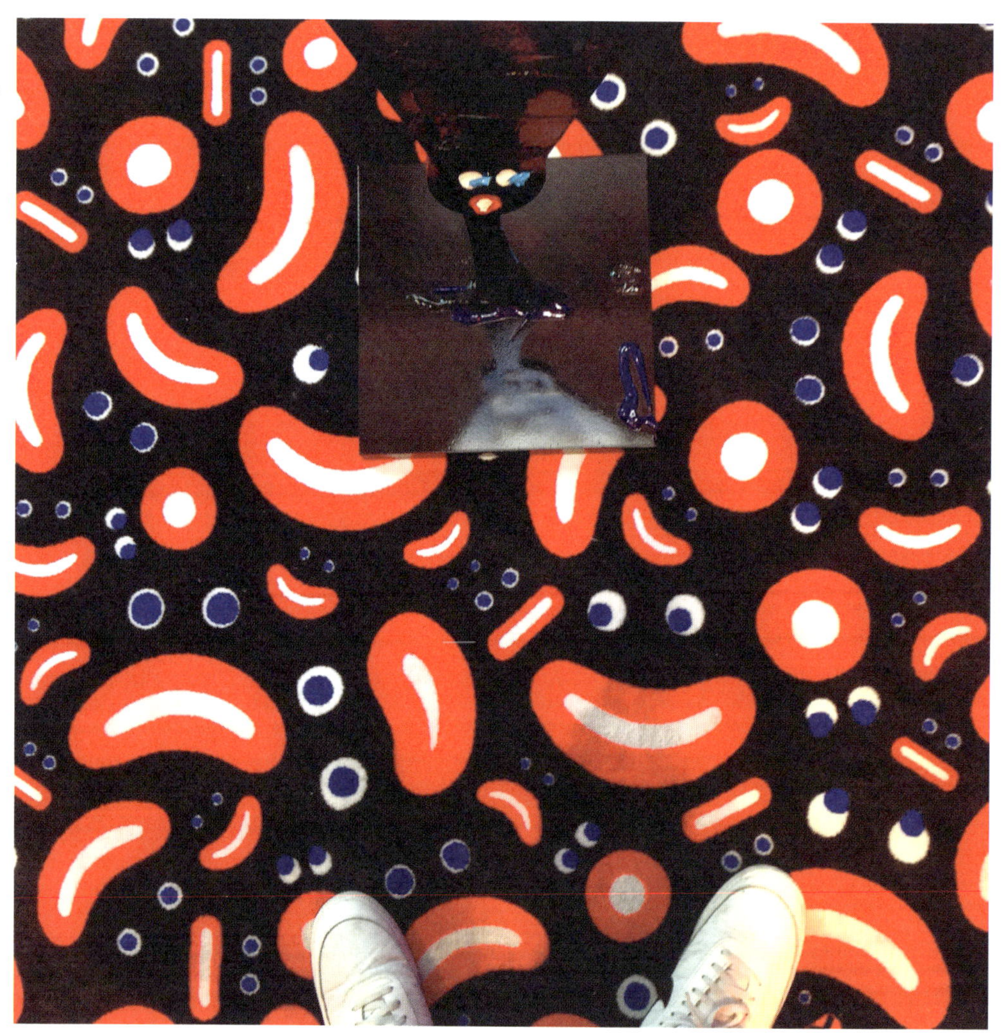

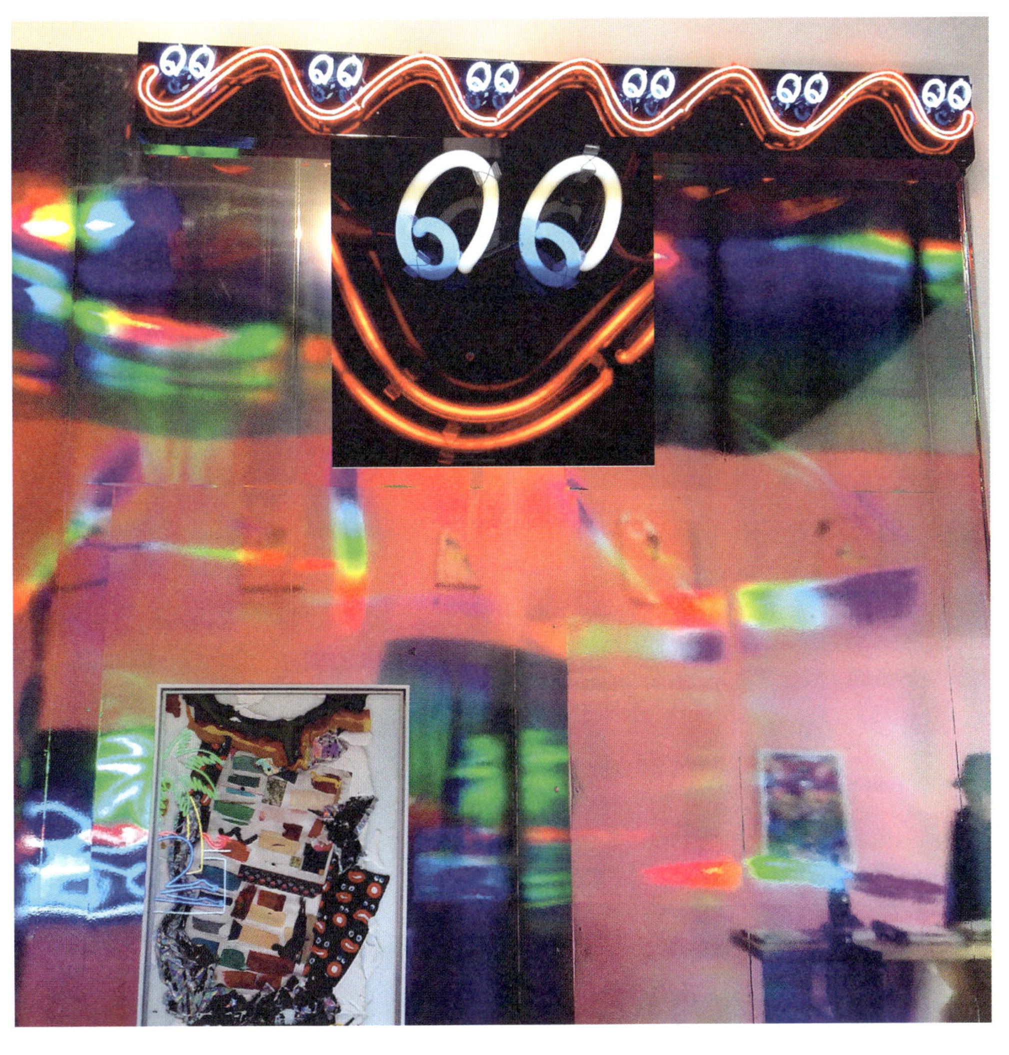

richard heller gallery
los angeles, 2015

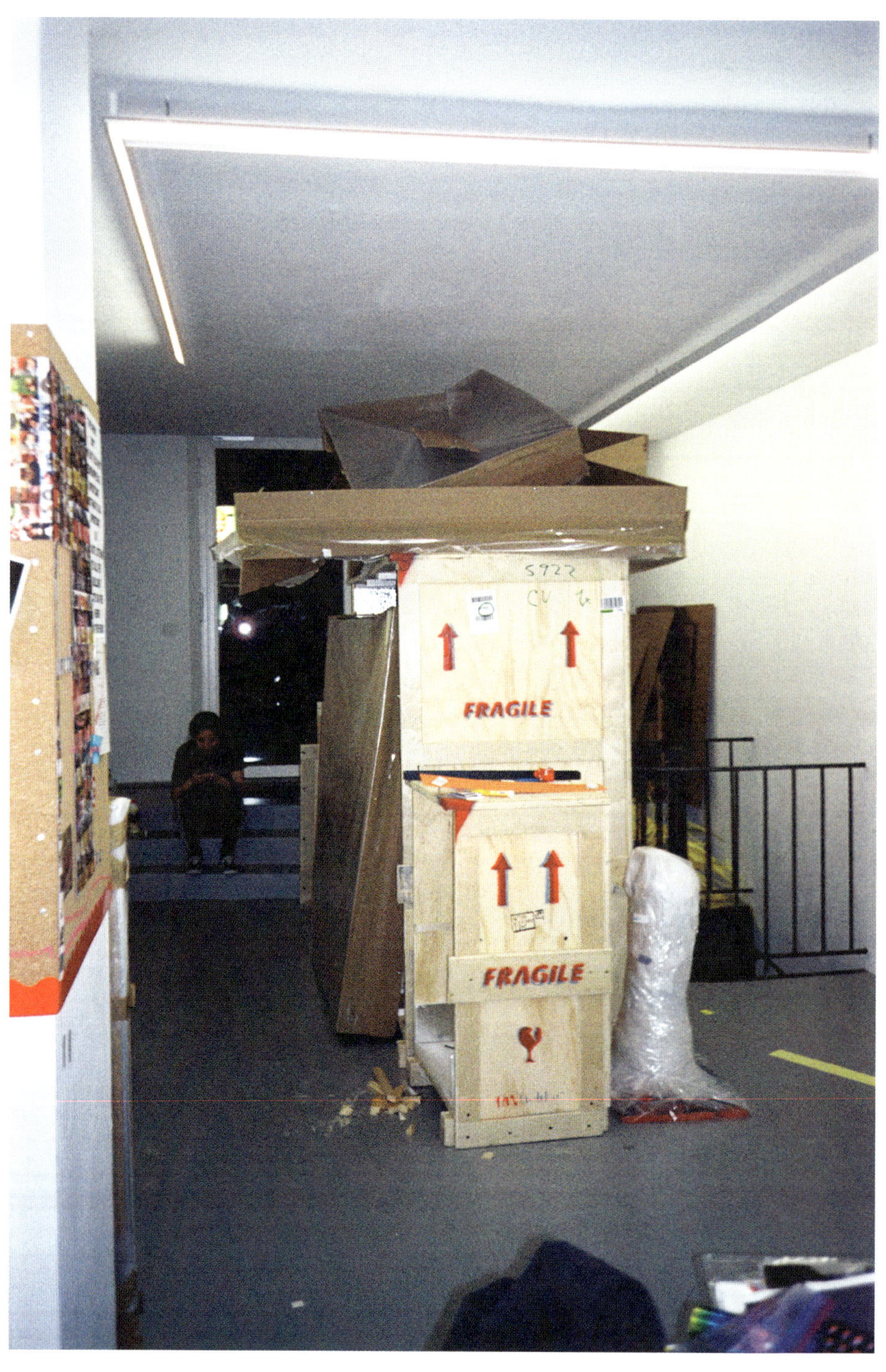

cologne, 2017

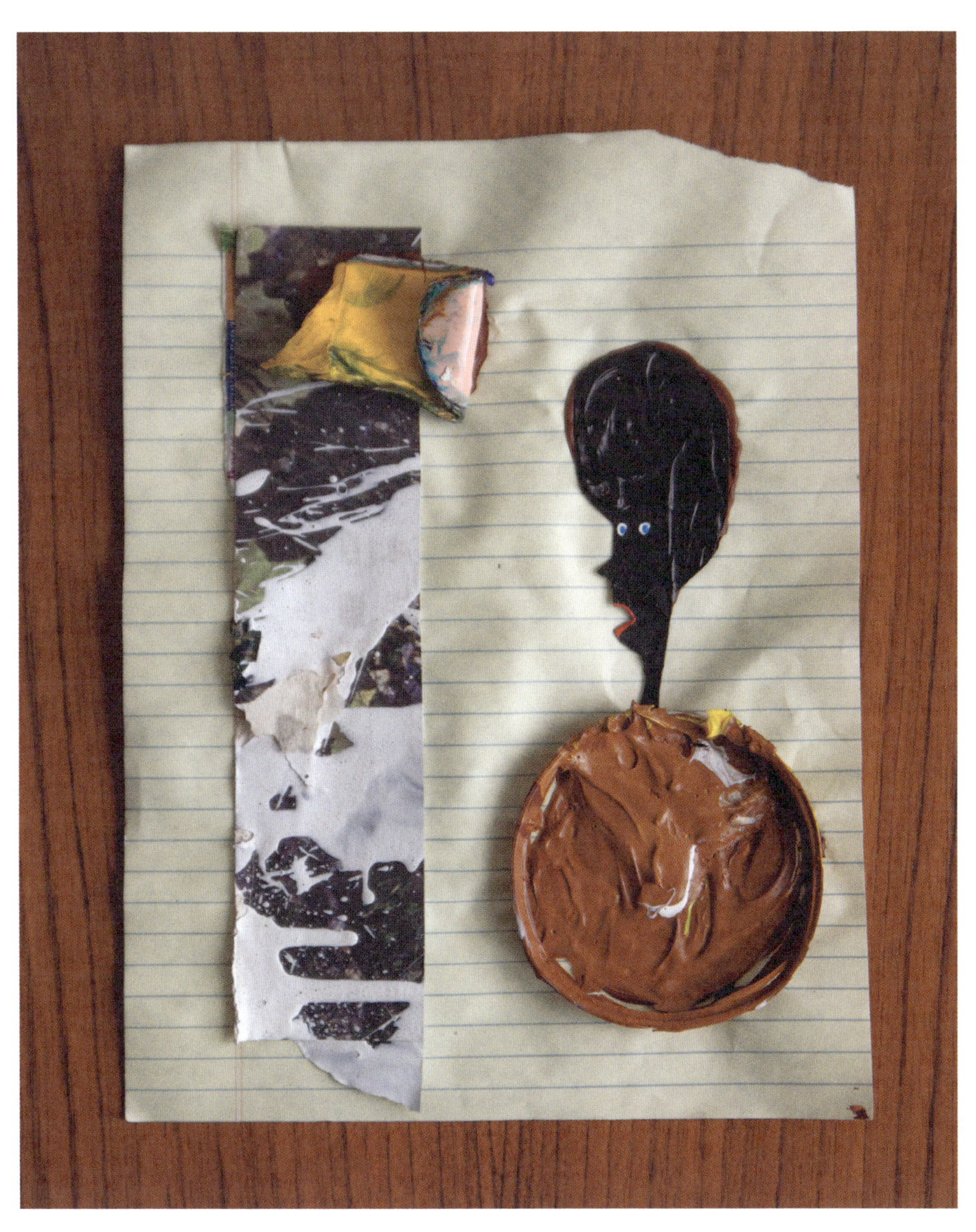

los angeles, 2018

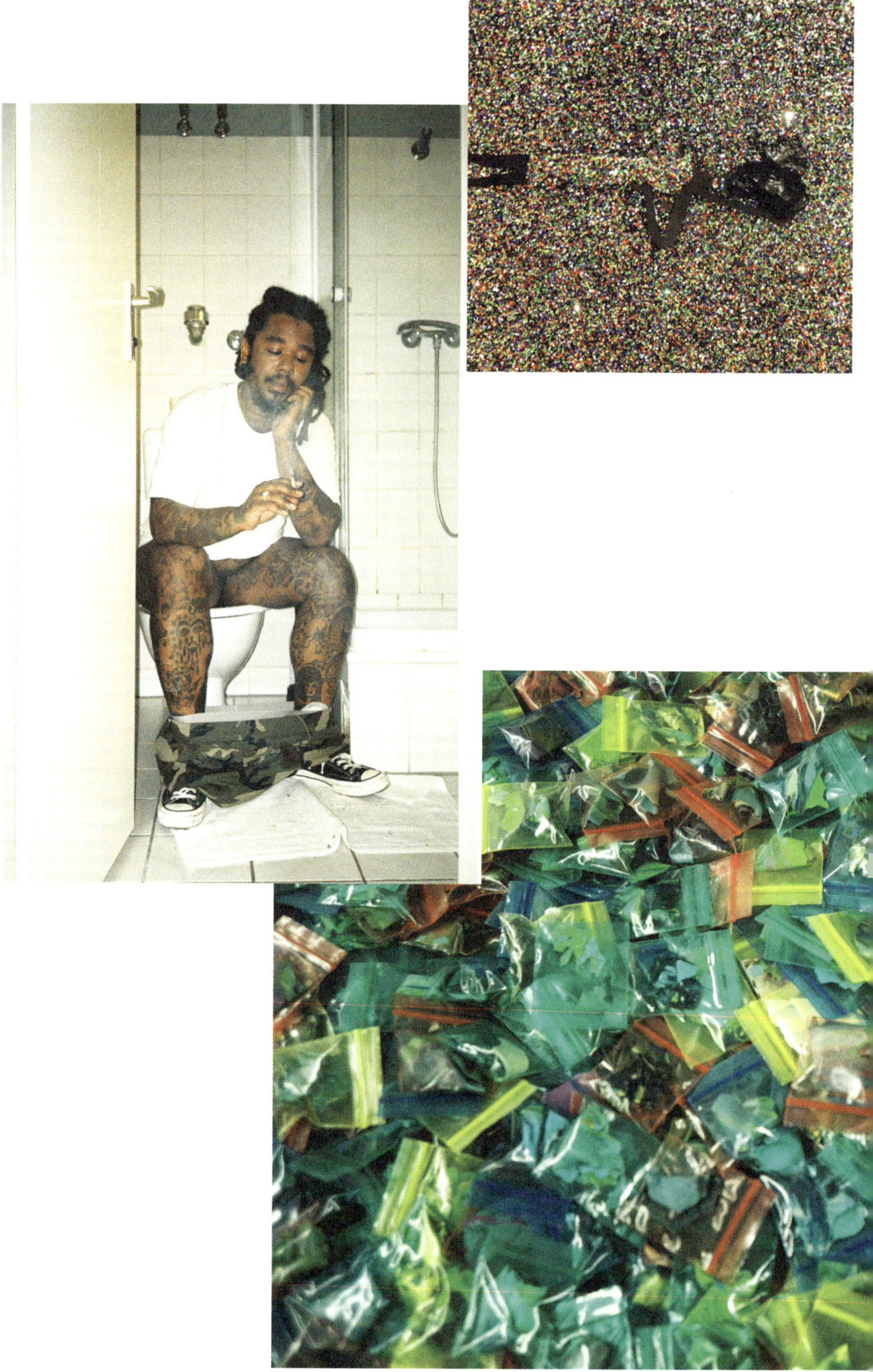

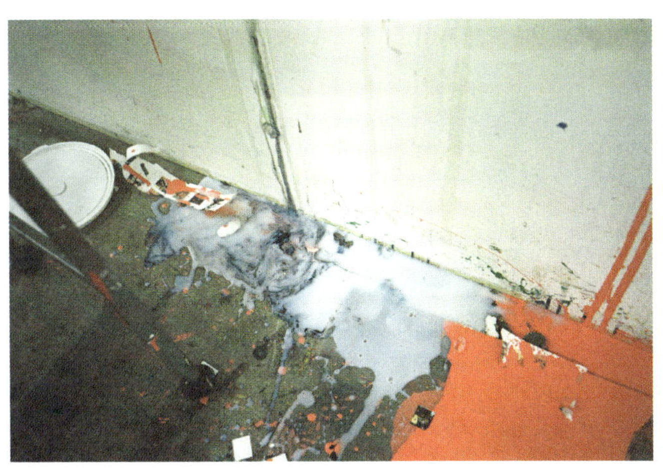

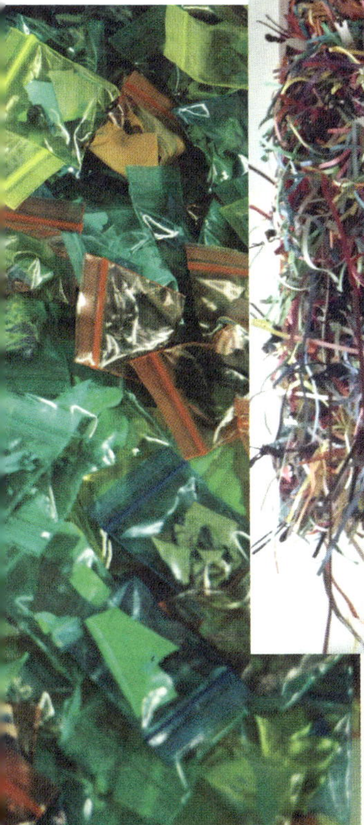

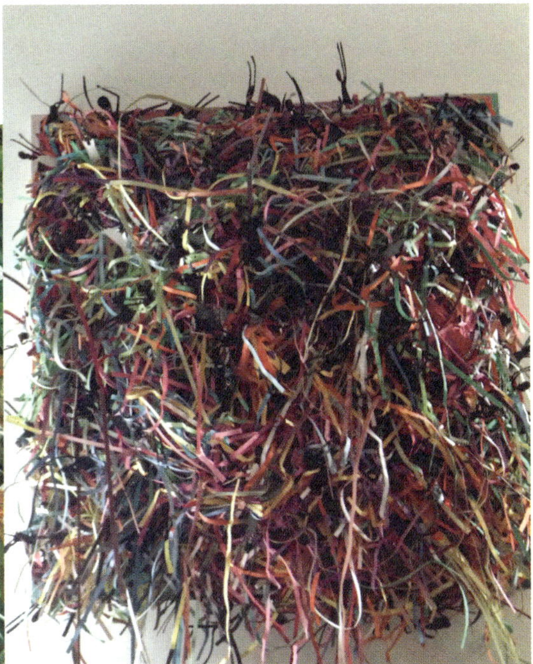

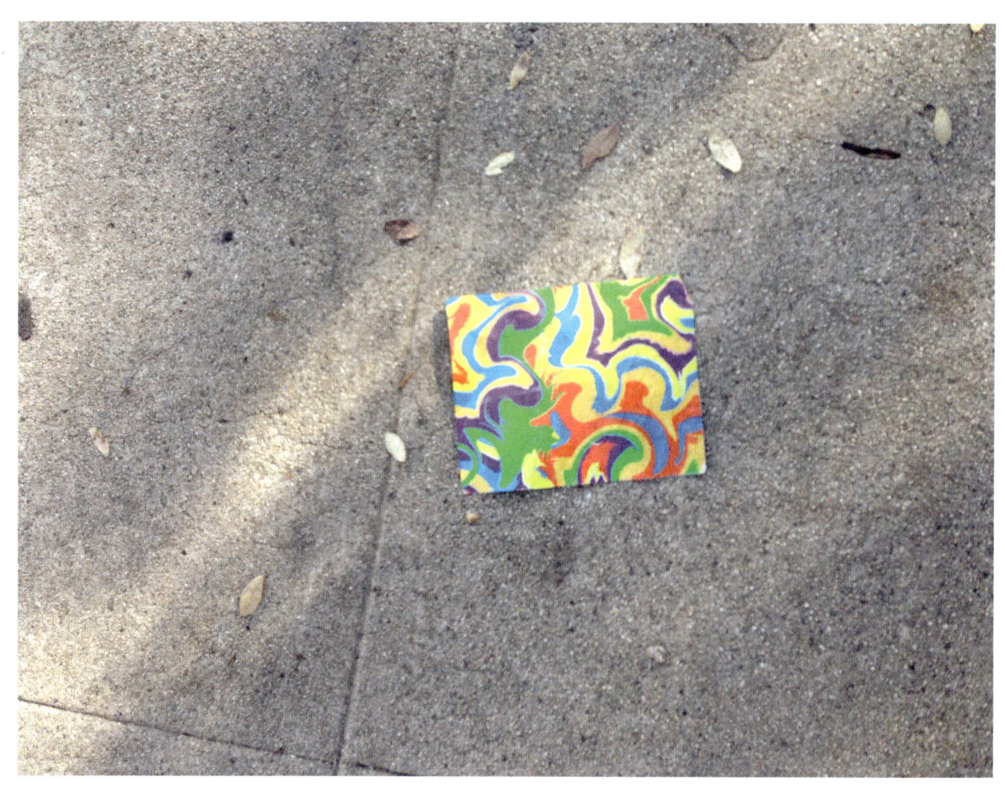

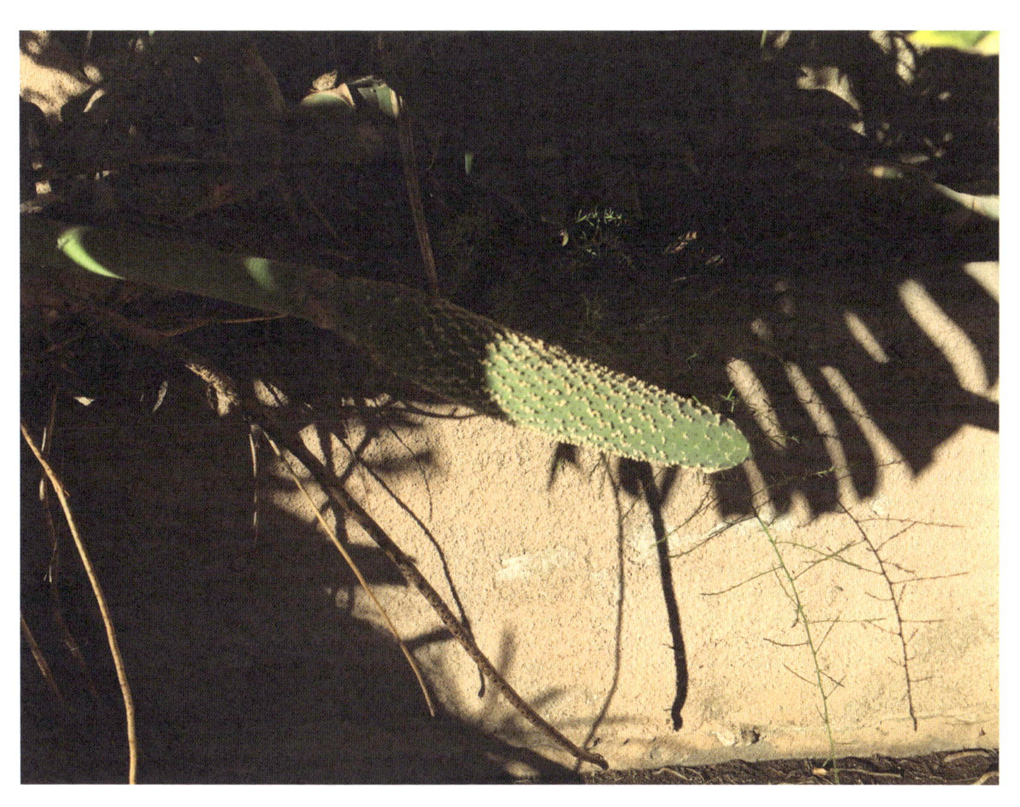

banana, pineapple, jackfruit

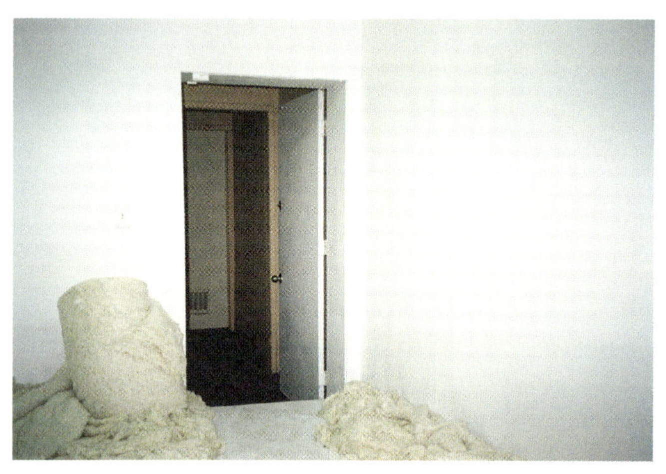

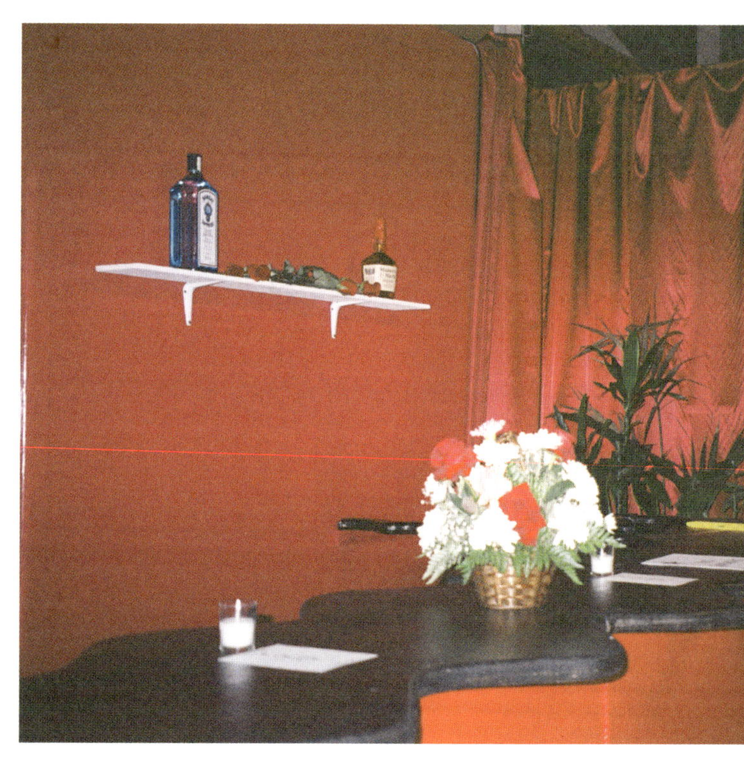

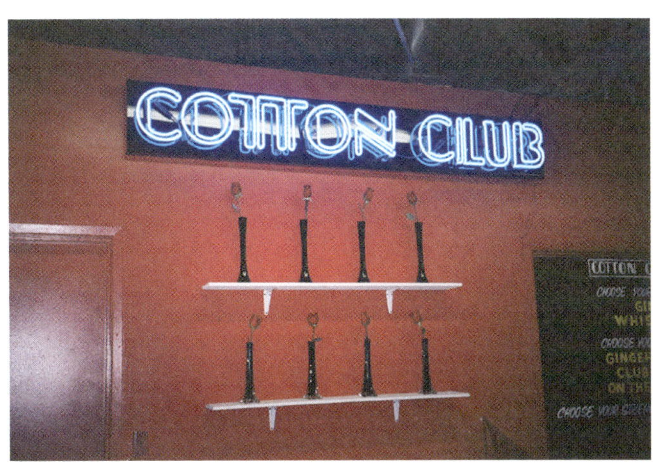

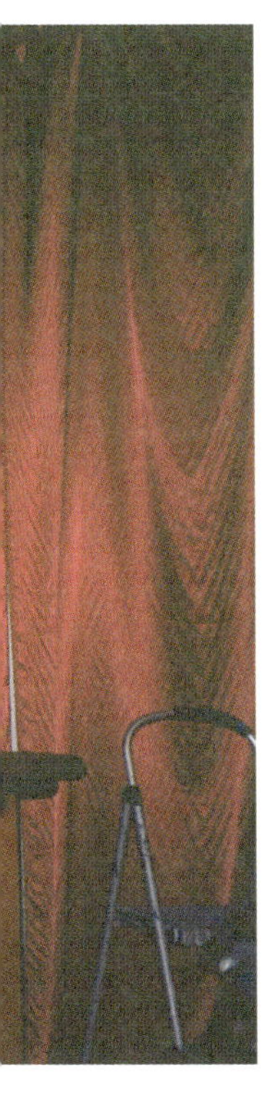

installation for Cotton Club at
Patrick Gomez 4 Sheriff, Los Angeles, 2016

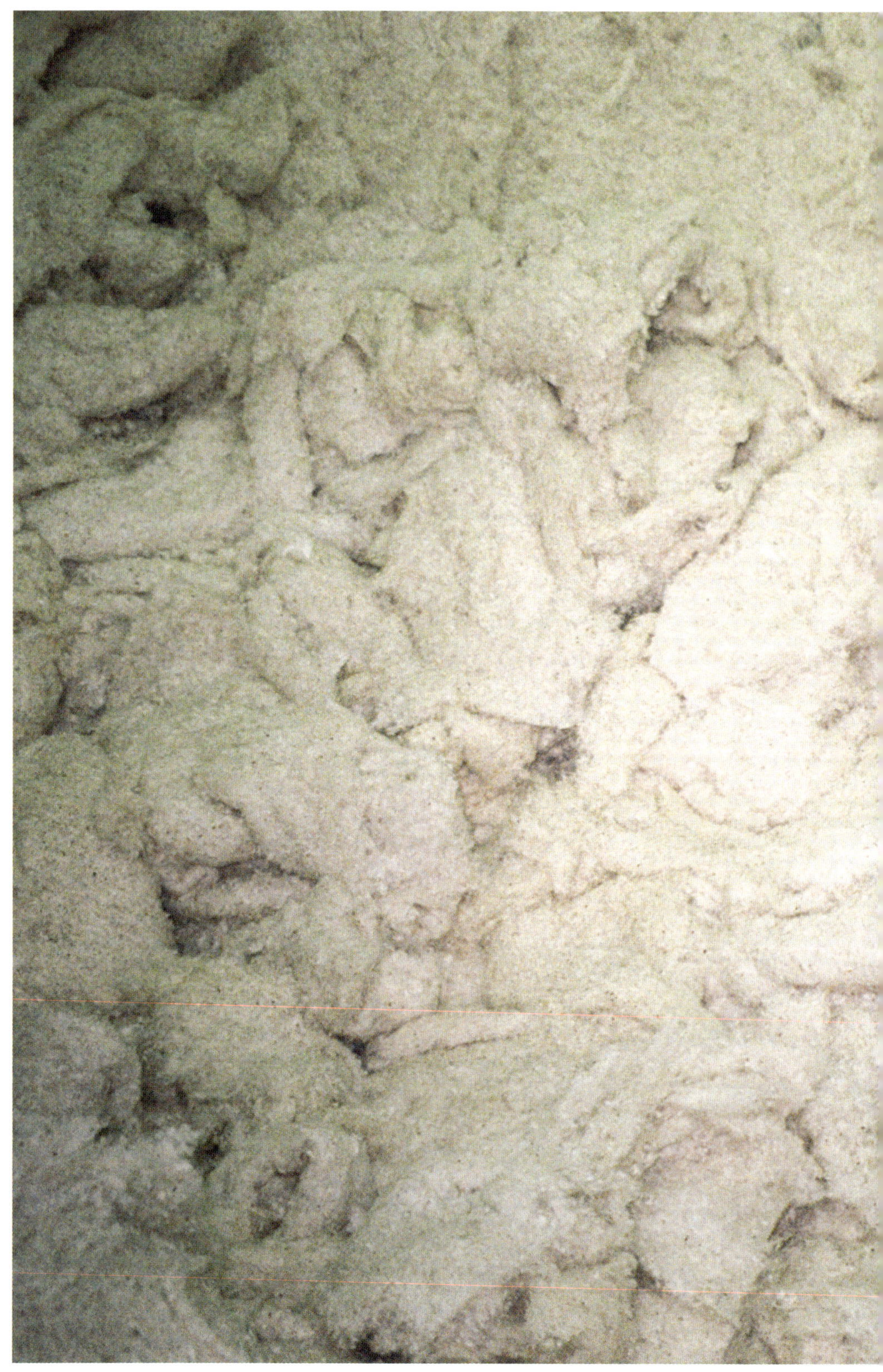

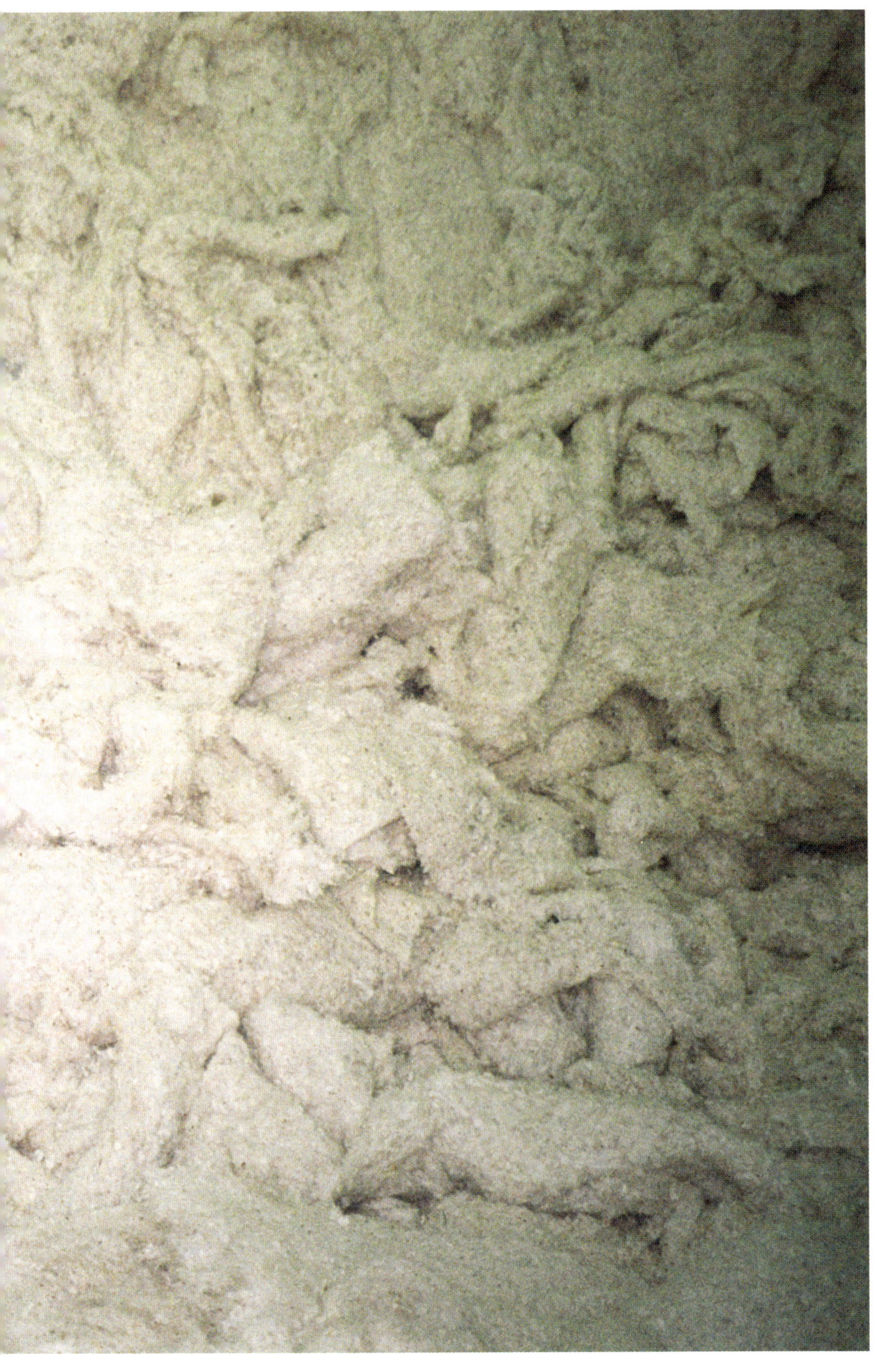

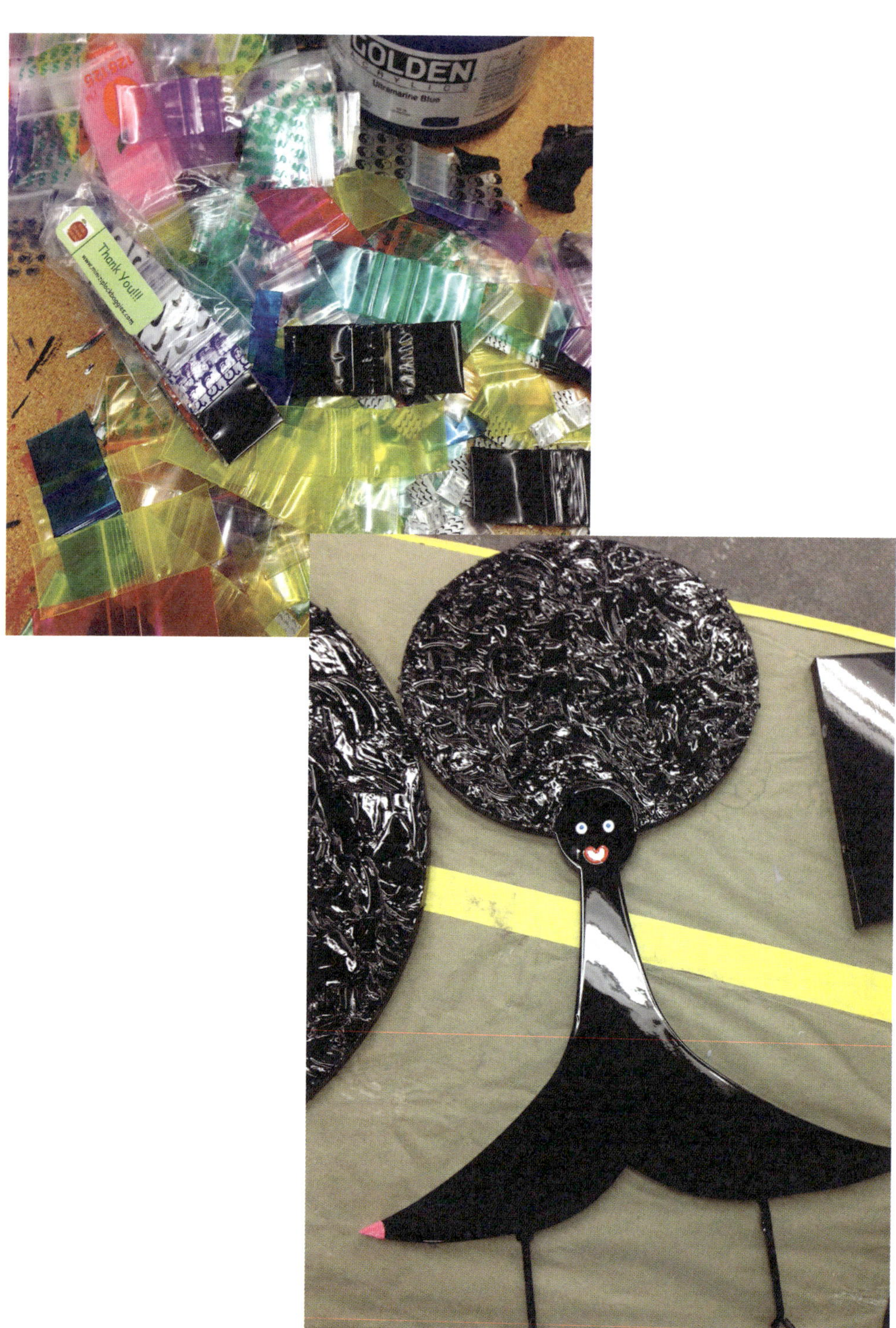
GOLDEN
Ultramarine Blue
Thank You!!!

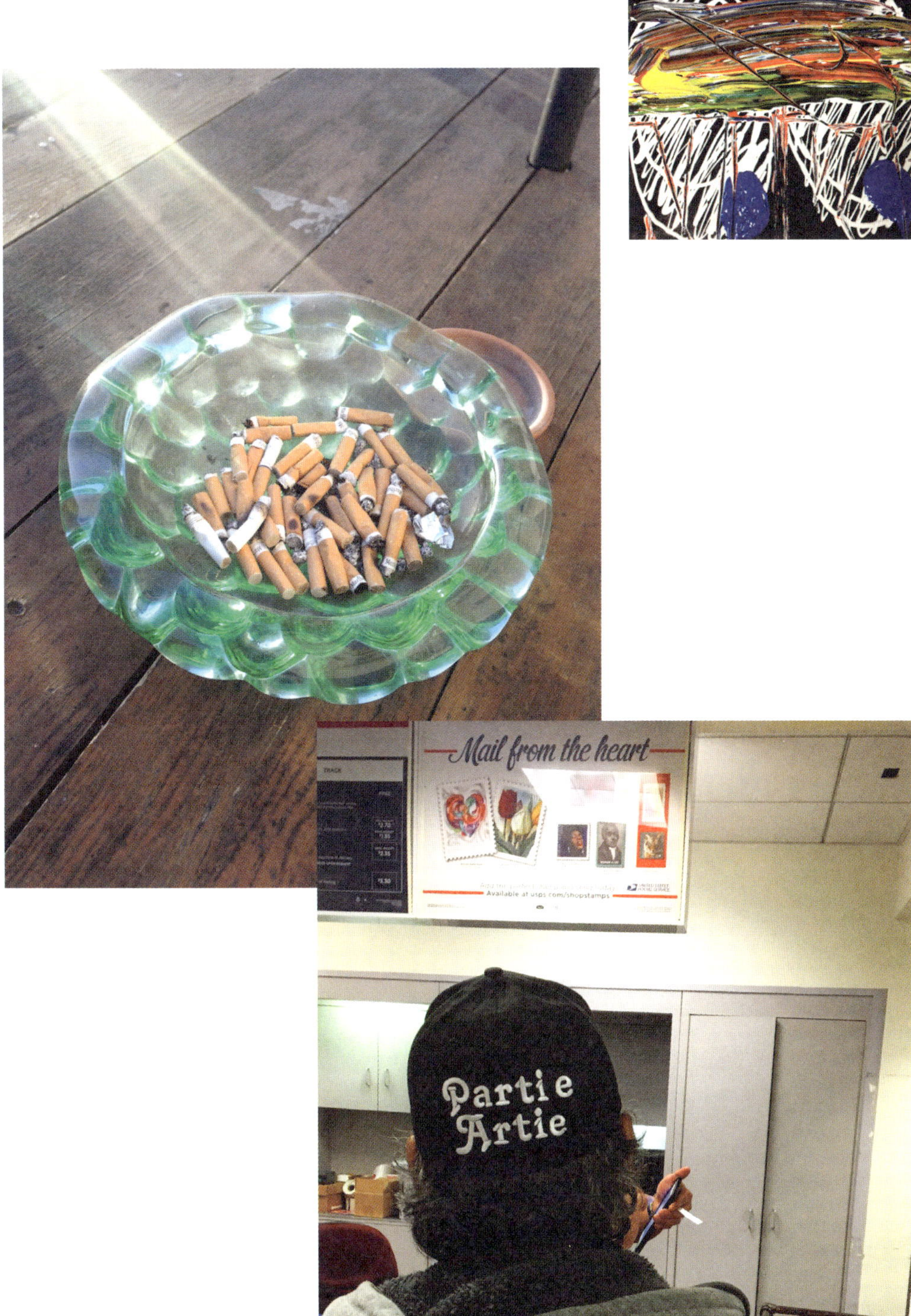
Mail from the heart
Available at usps.com/shopstamps
Partie
Artie

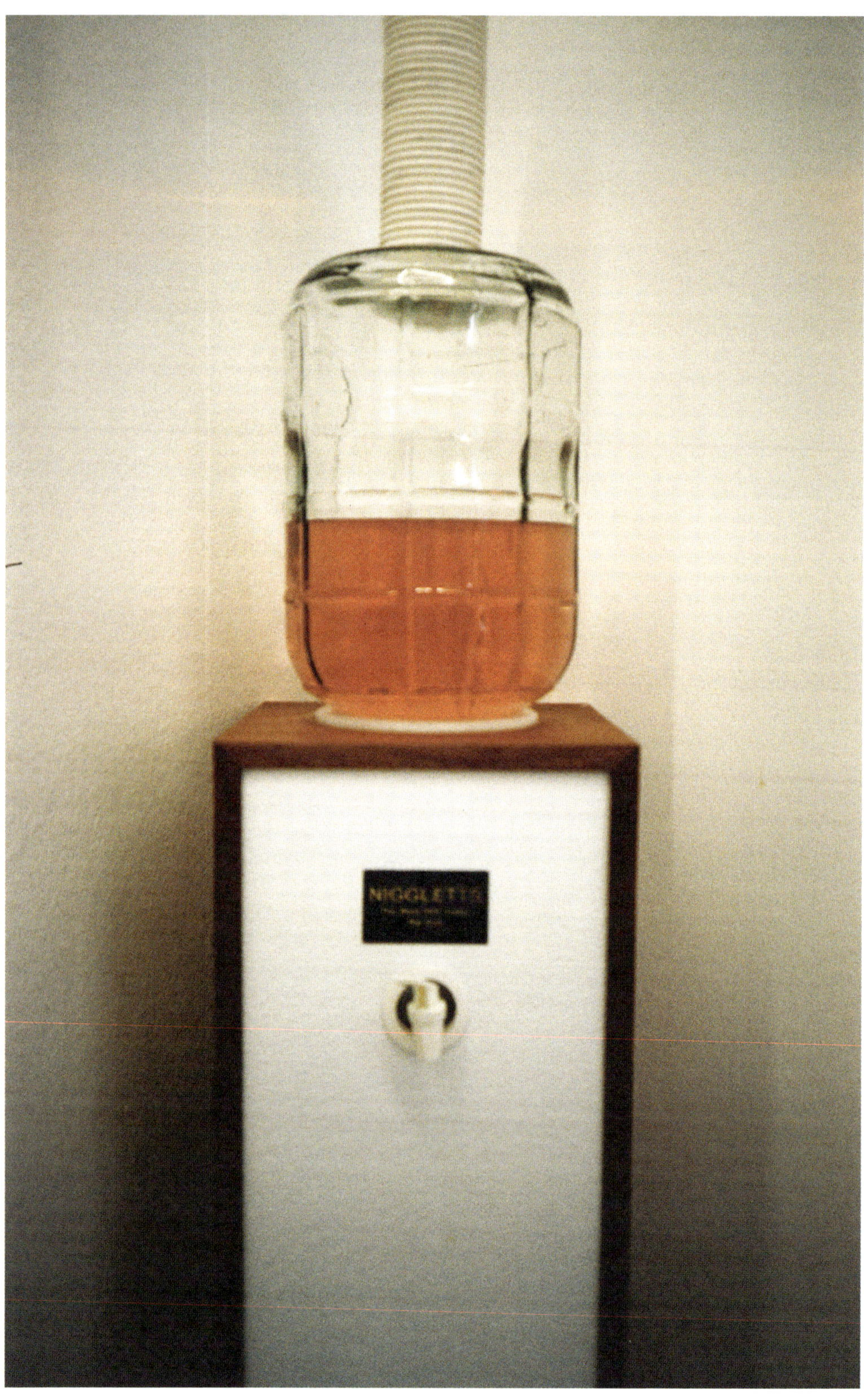

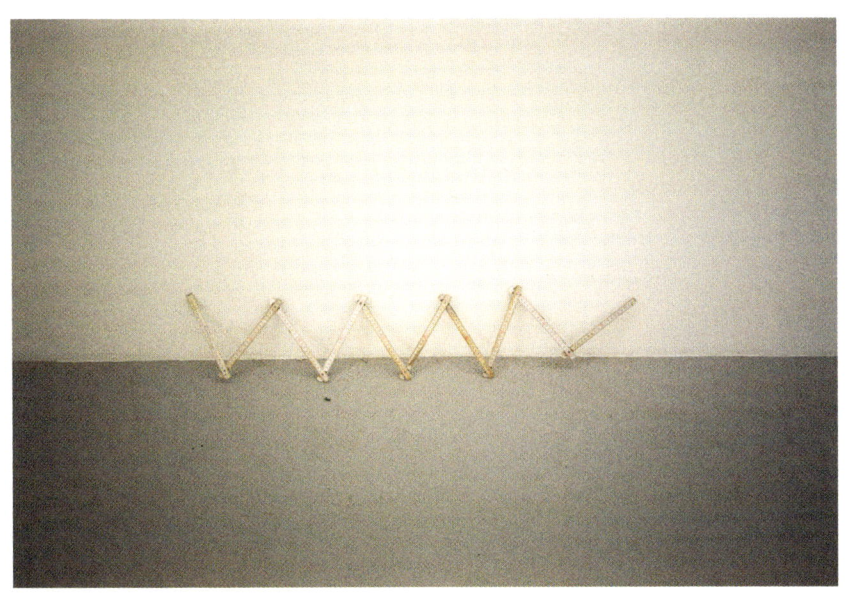

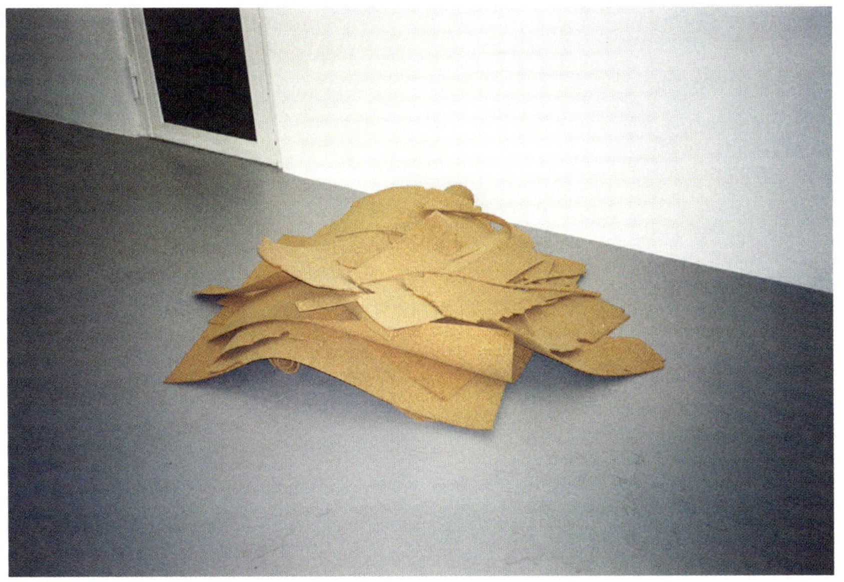

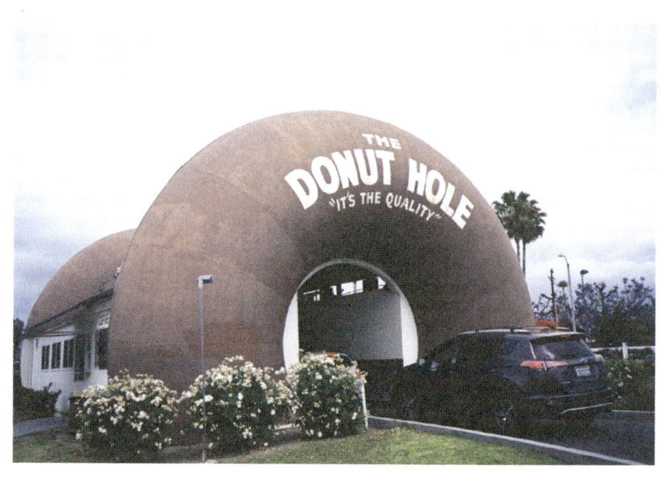
THE
DONUT HOLE
"IT'S THE QUALITY"

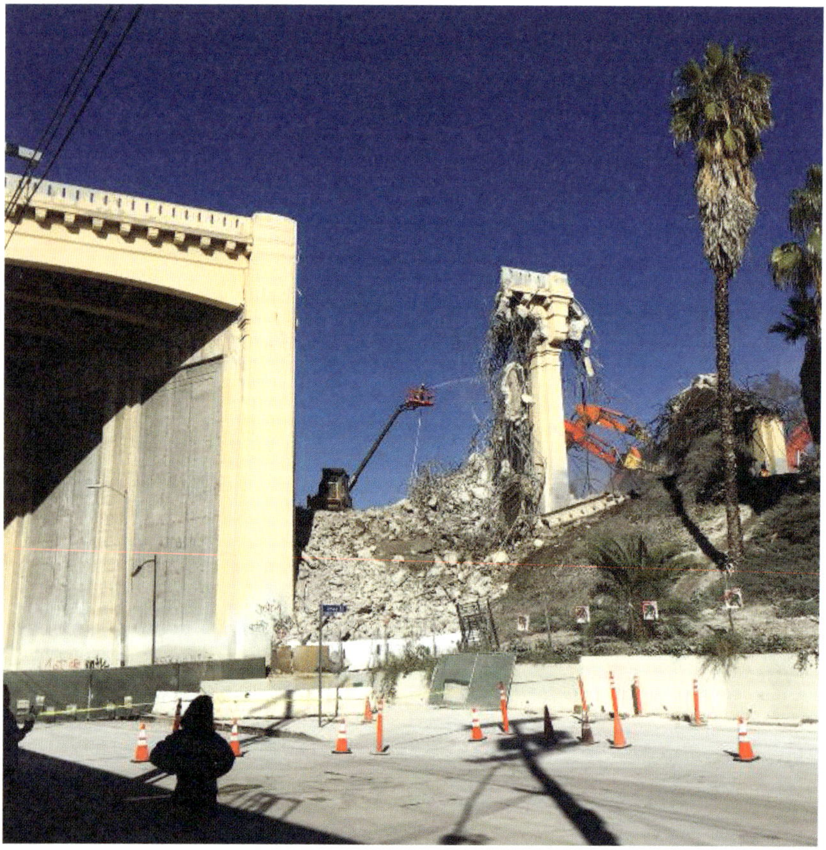

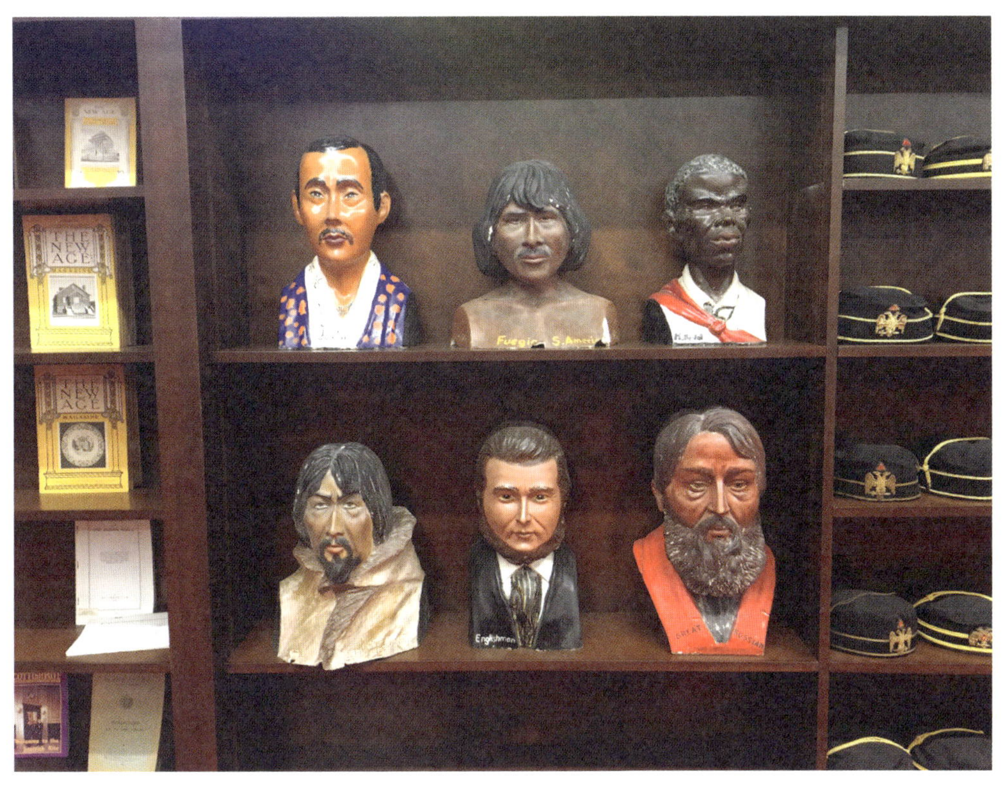

everyone i know has a david hammons story

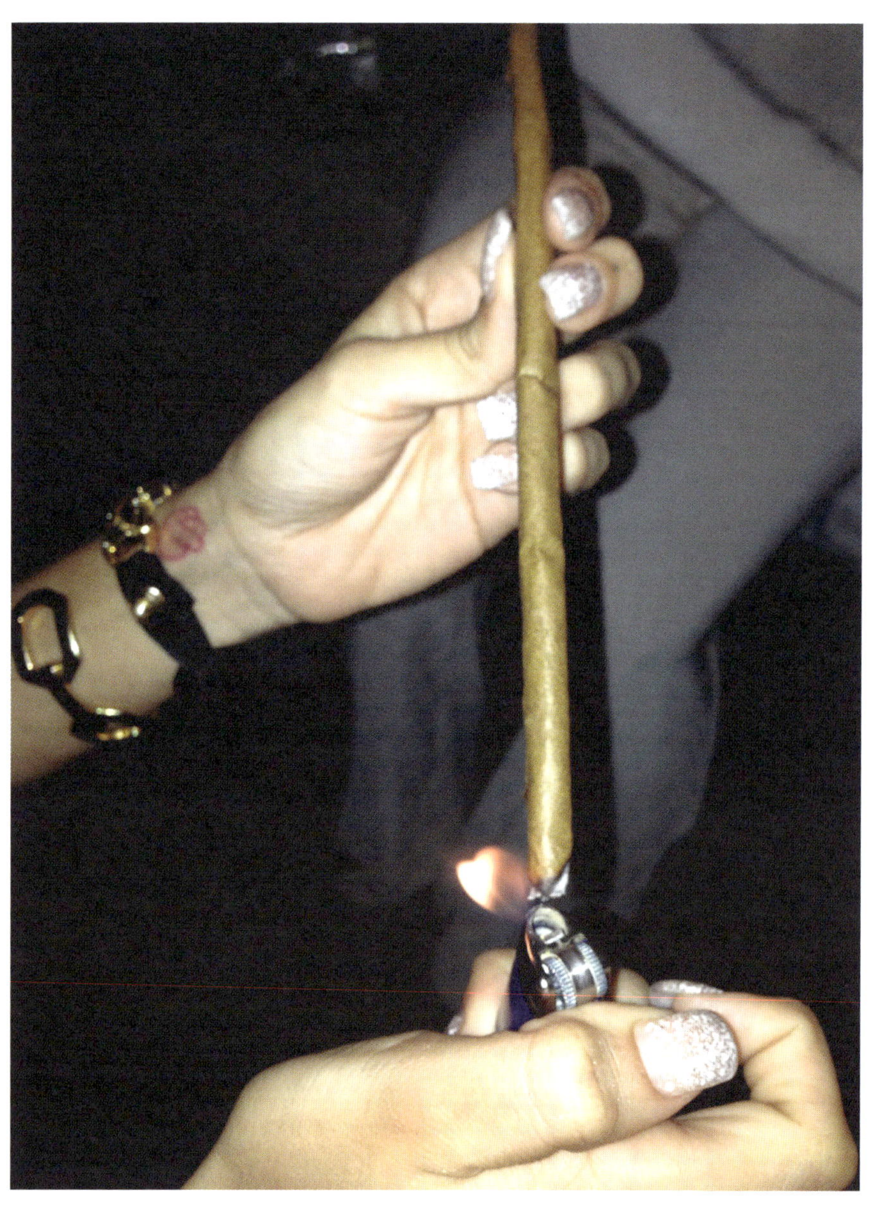

extendo cliip

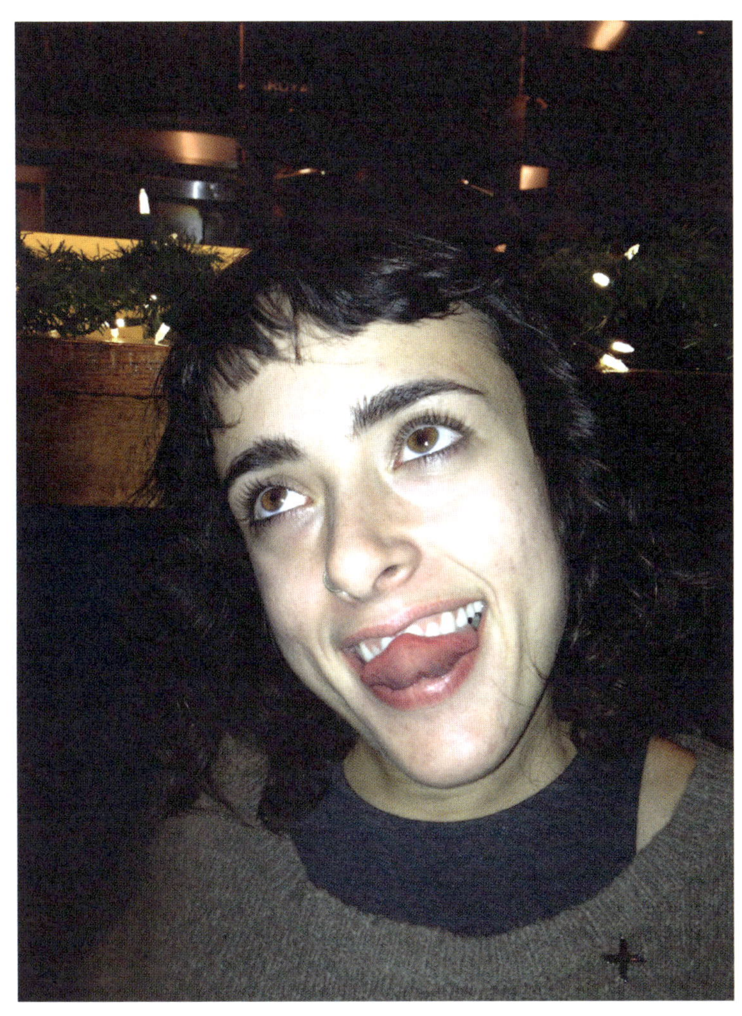

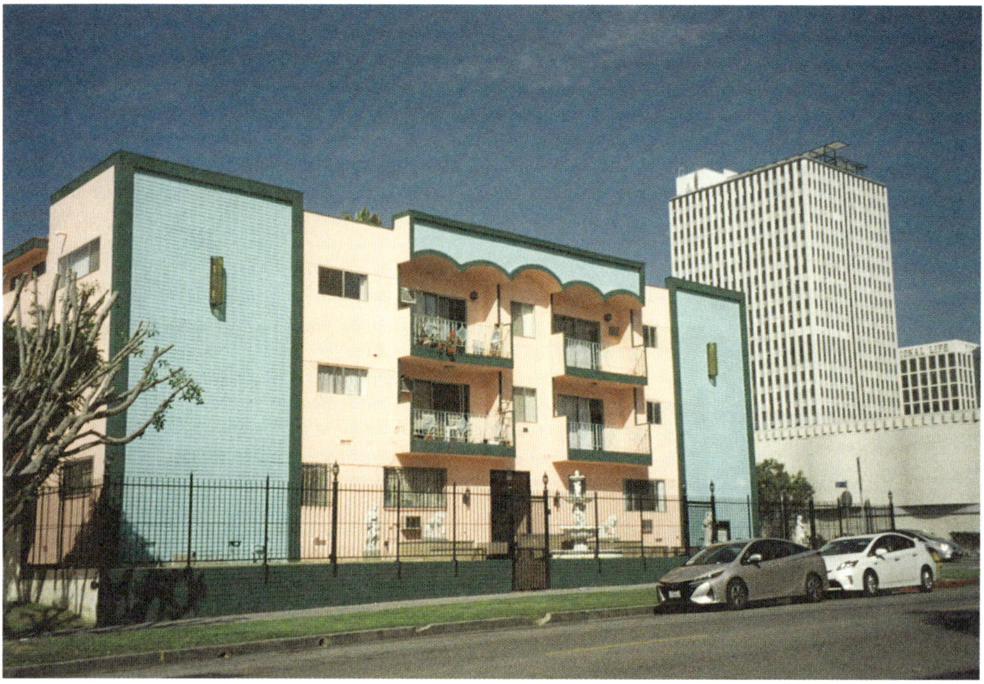

home, 2015

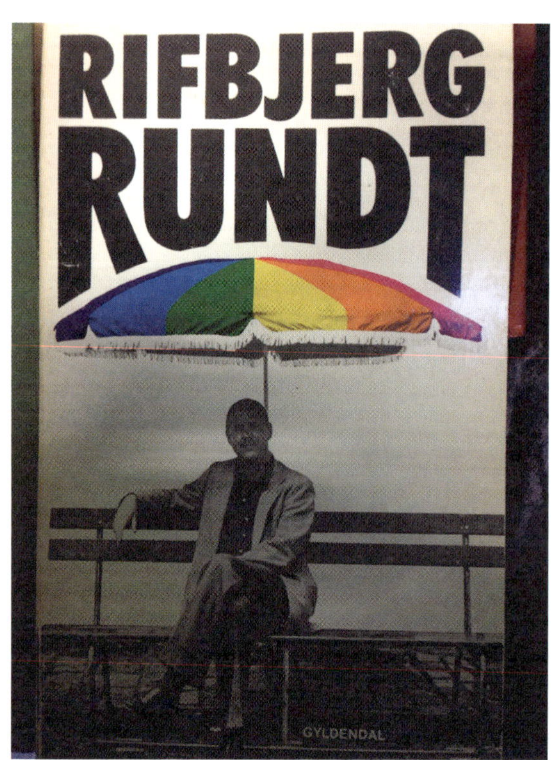

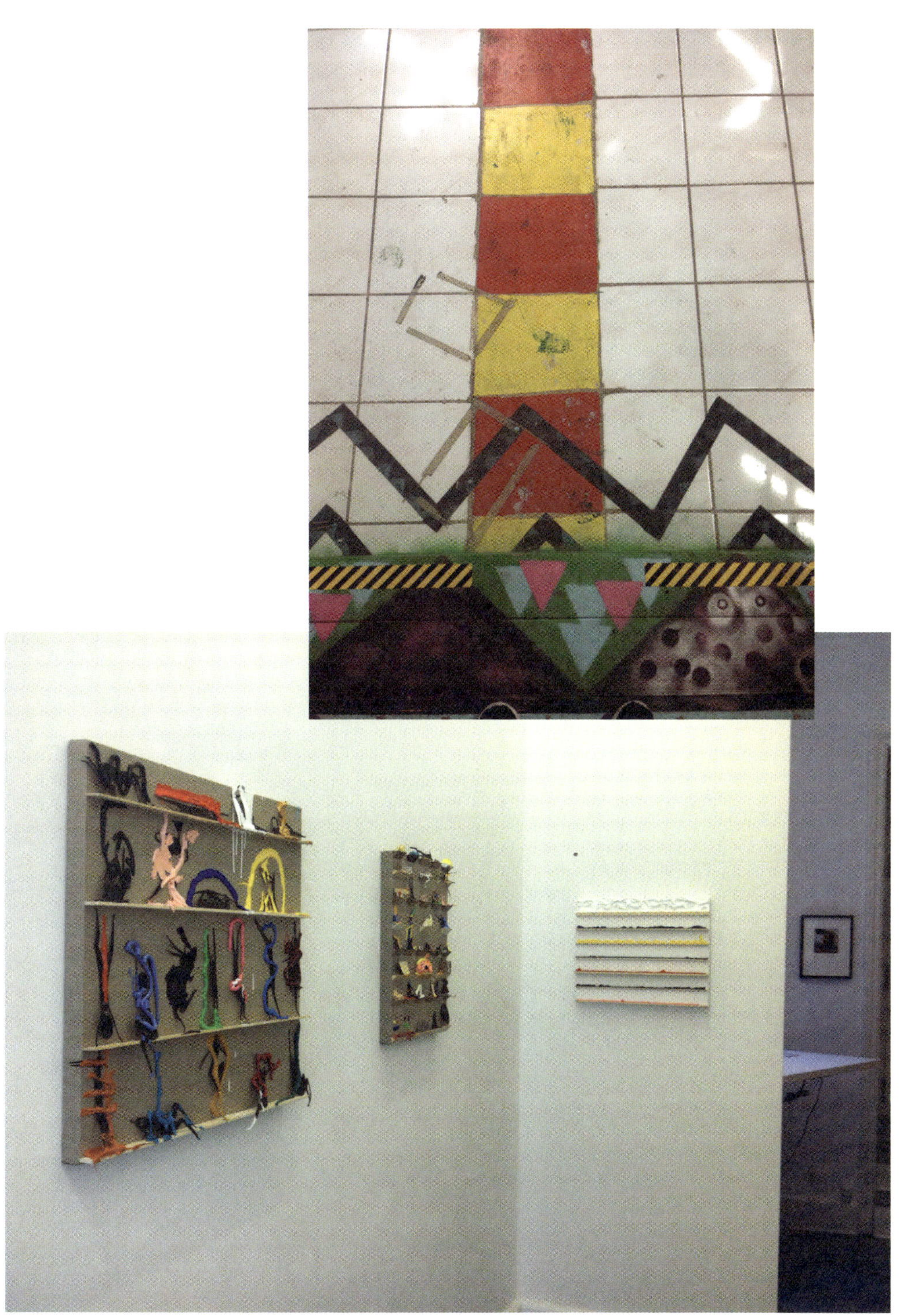

copenhagen, 2013?

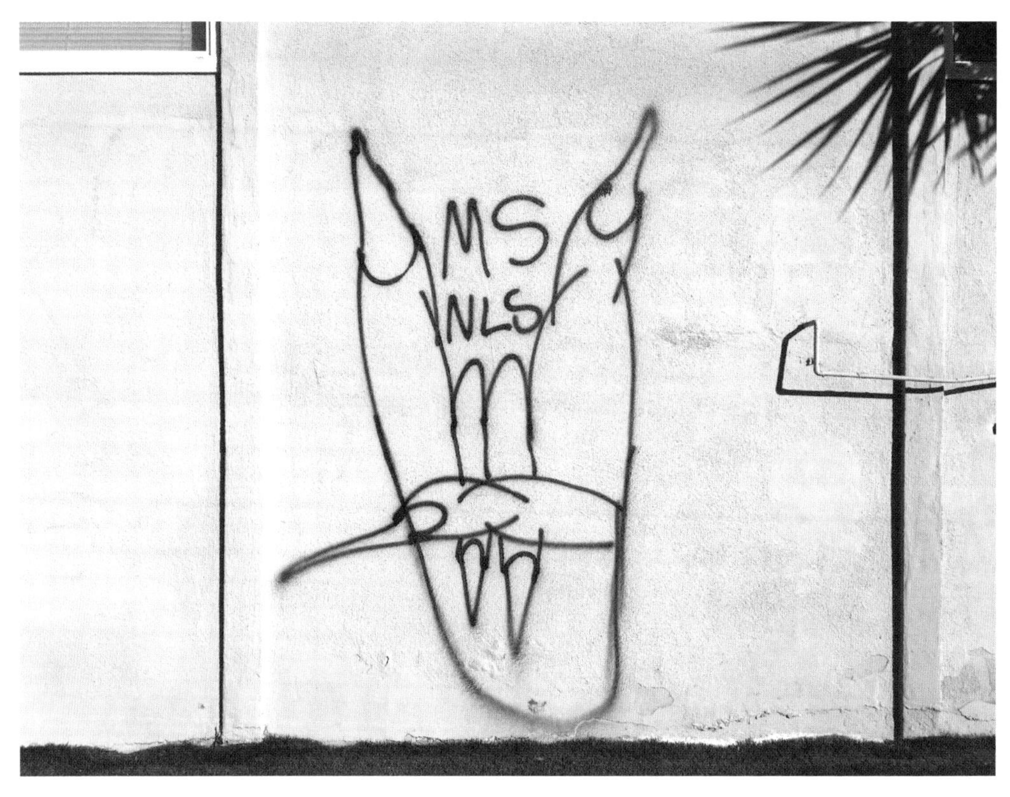

a sign one makes with their hands in representation of what set or hood they are from

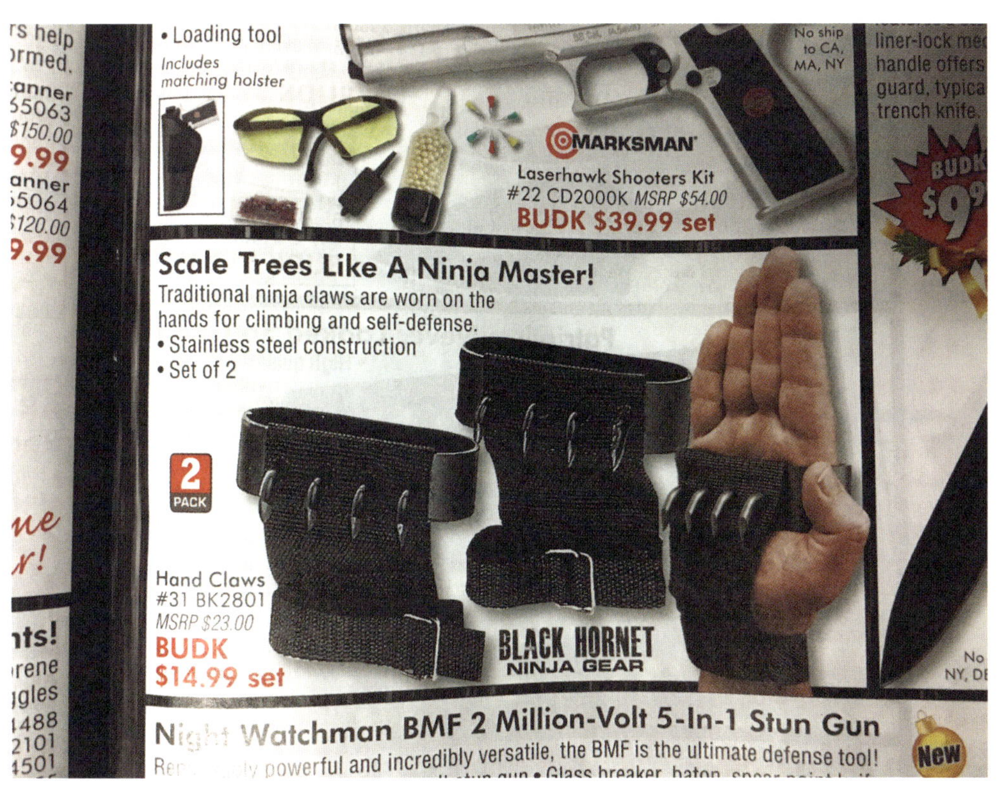

see dat fool, don't he know he shouldn't be
throwin them signs up round hurre

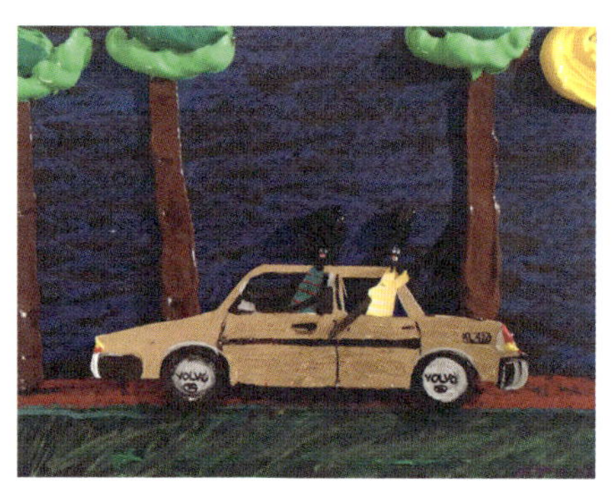

two niggas in a volvo,
2014

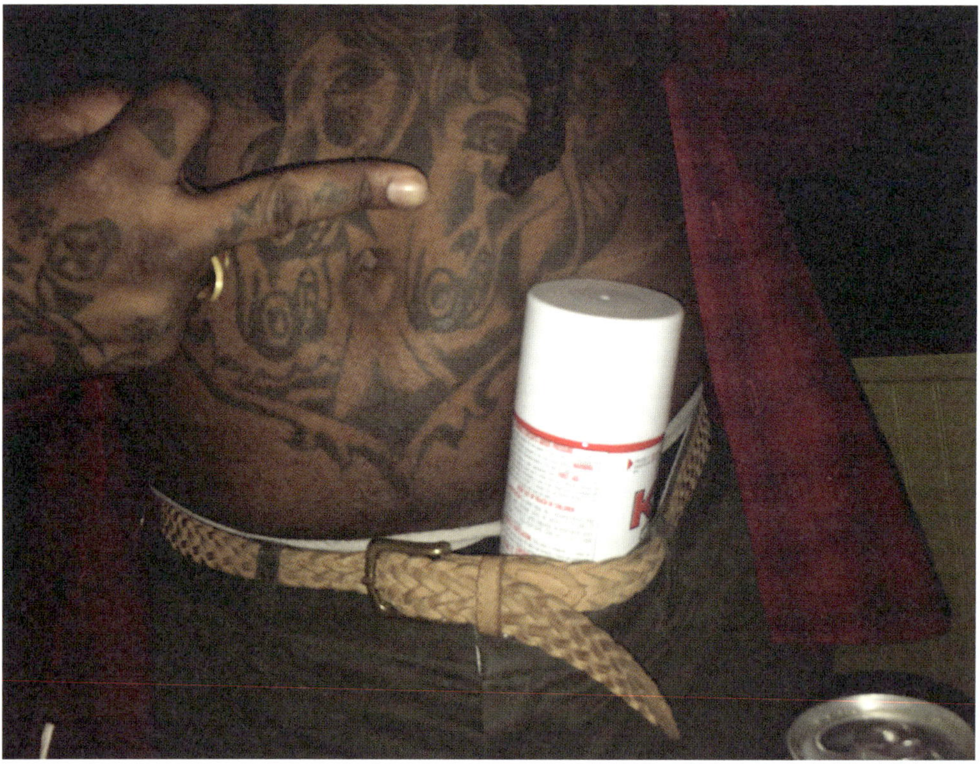

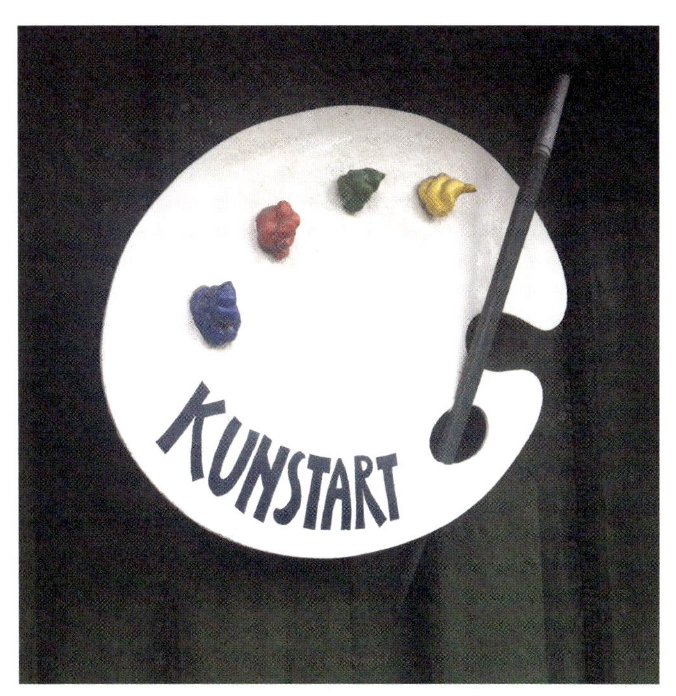
KUNSTART

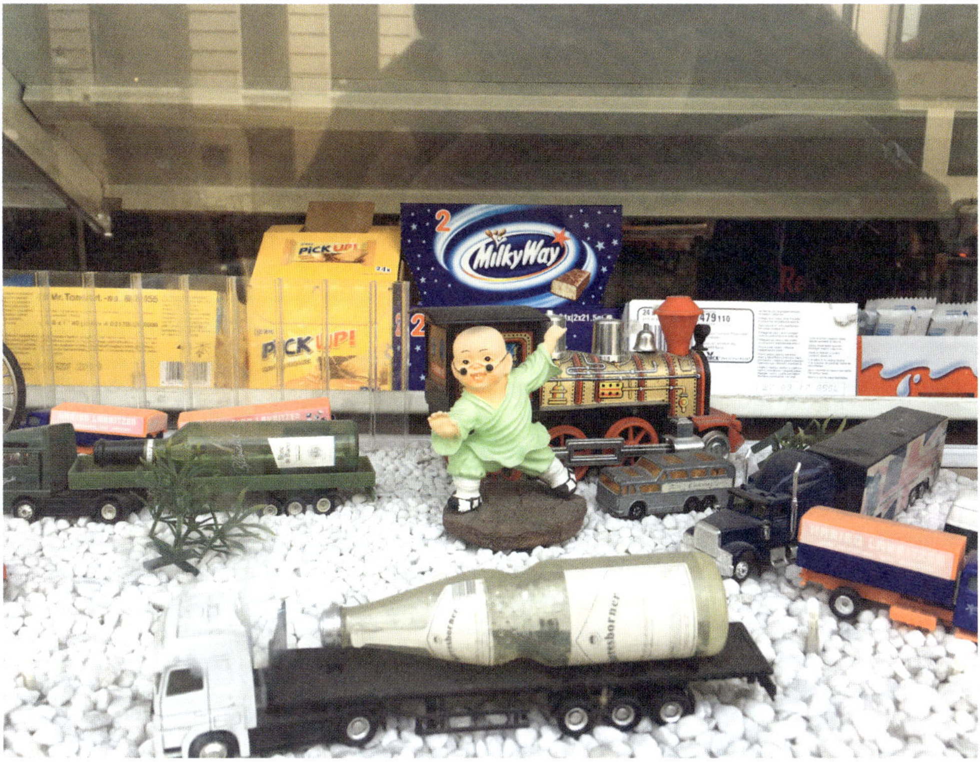

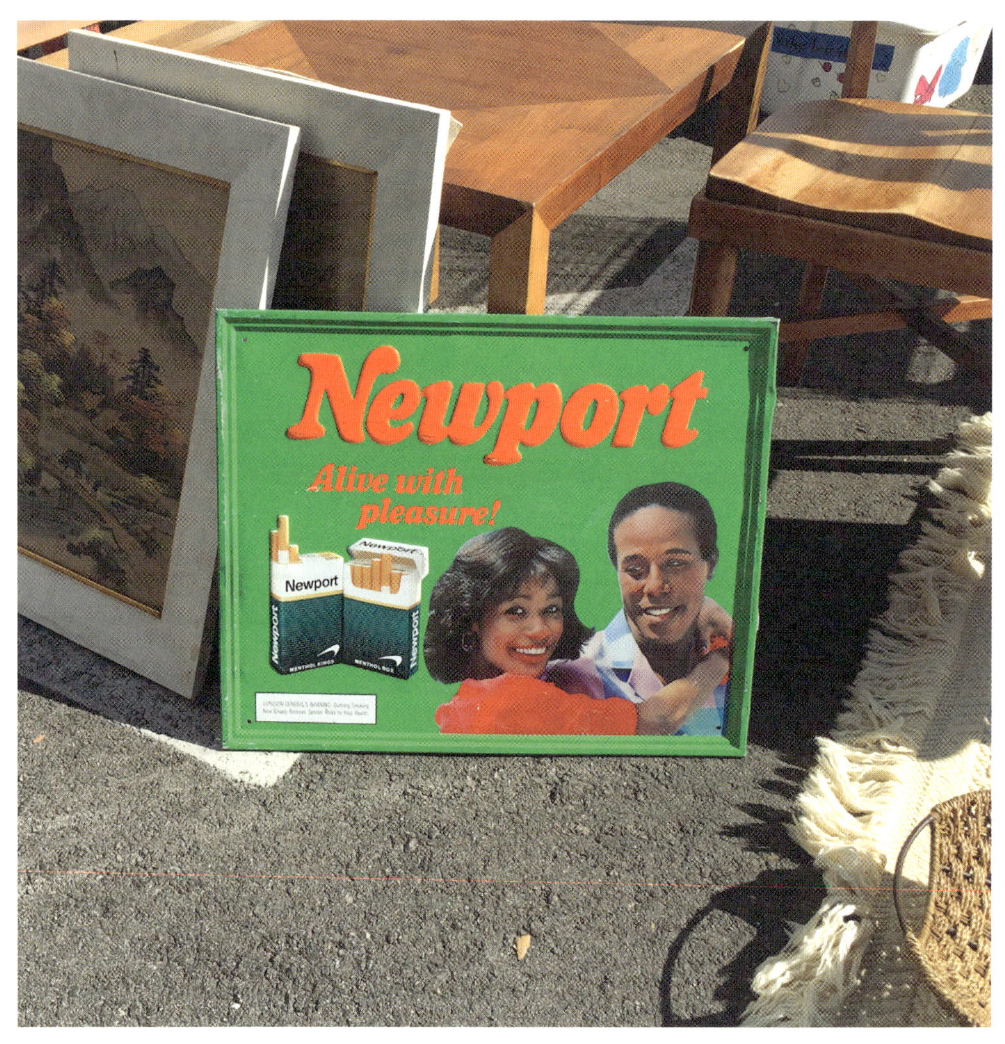

losing you is not all i lost this time

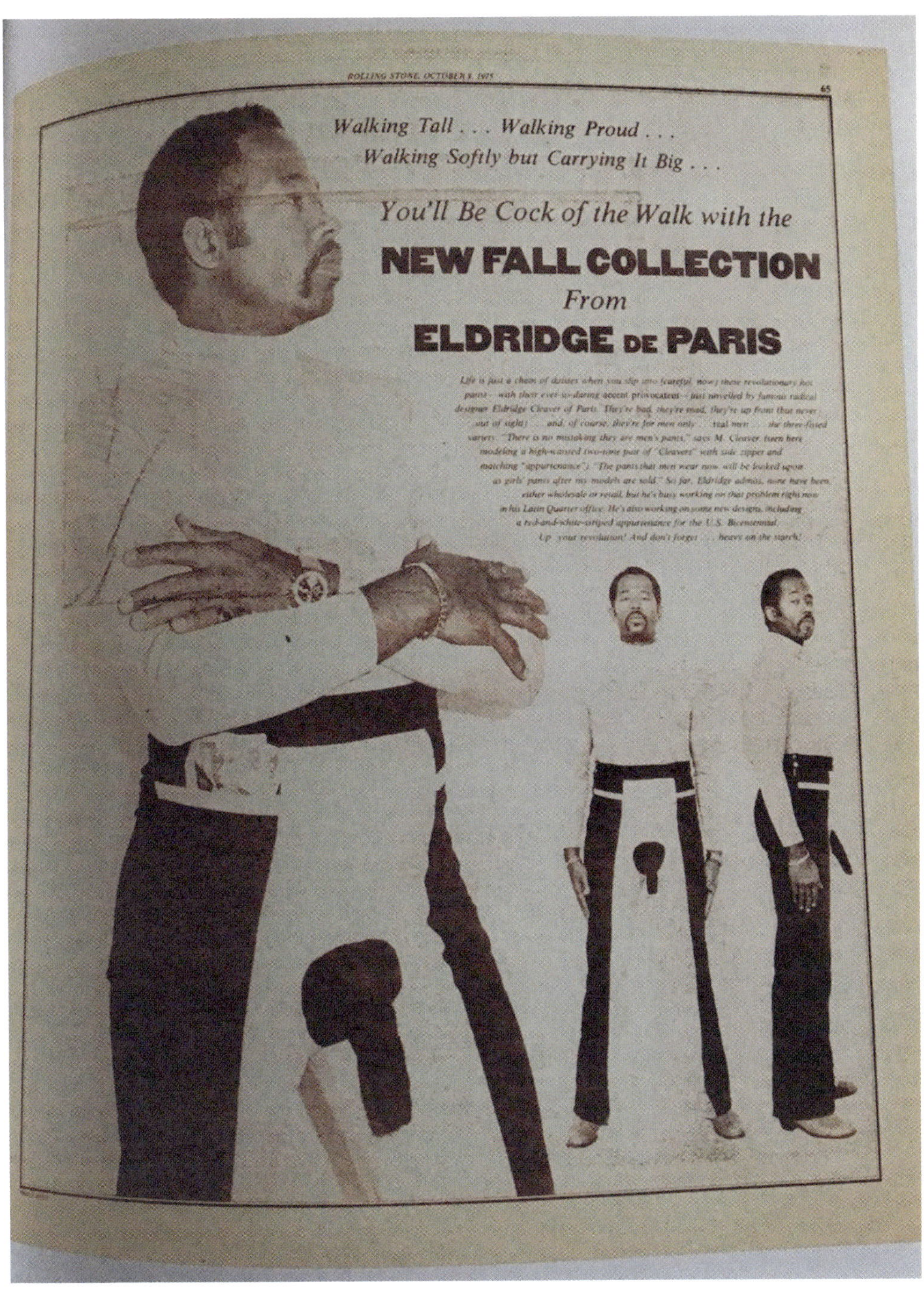

does it hurt so bad (you make it hurt so bad)
tell me why (why, why)

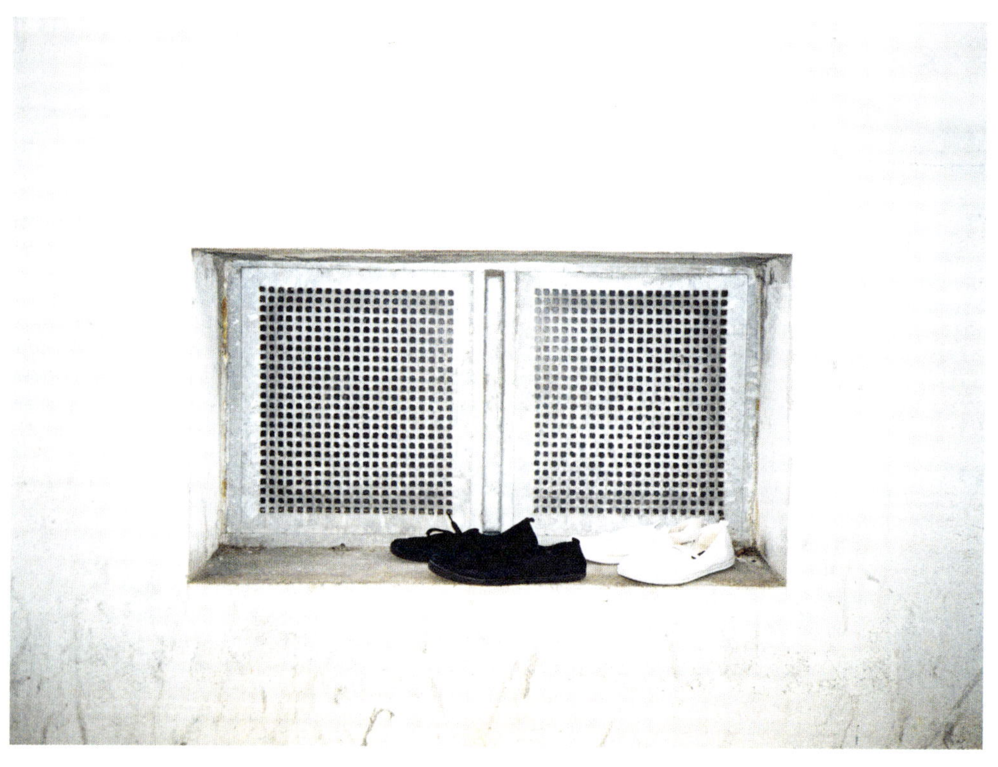

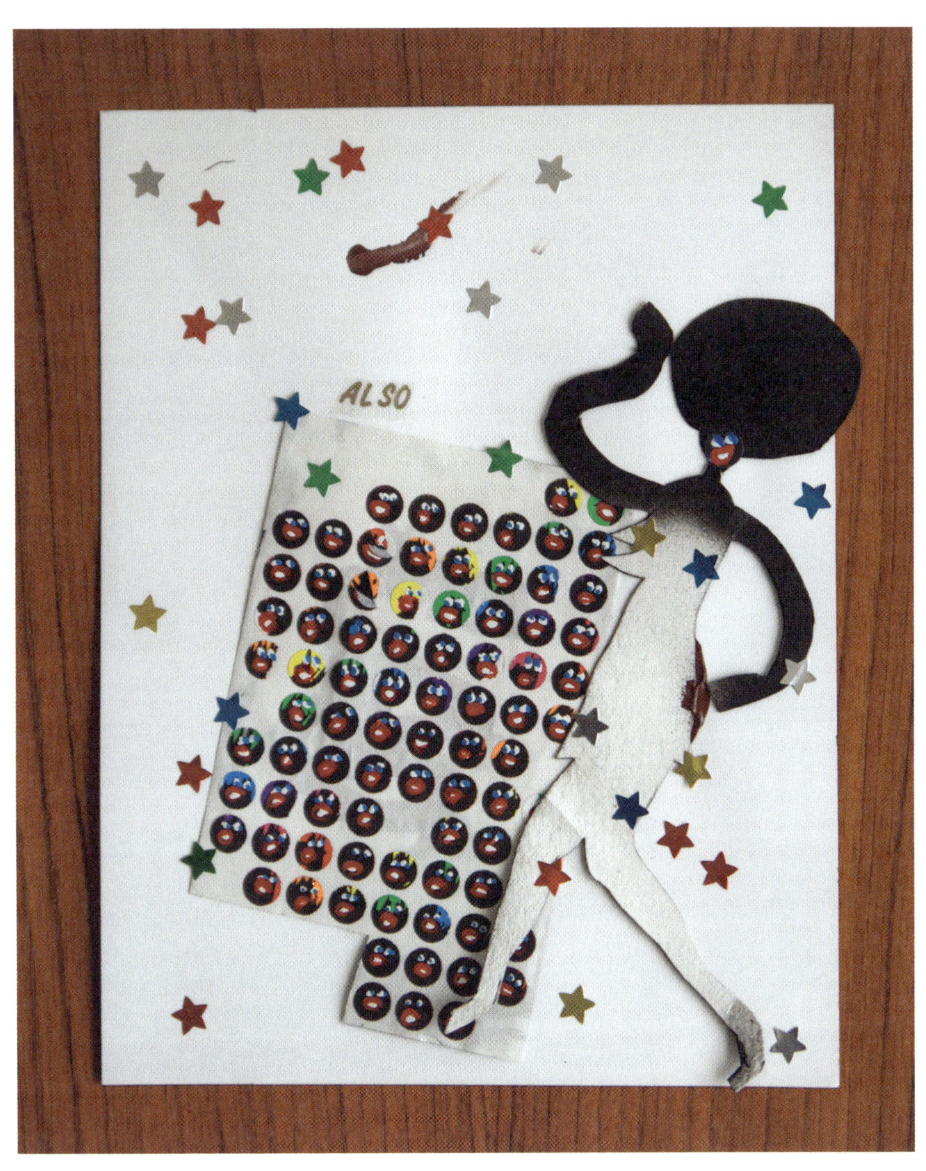

stars and dots

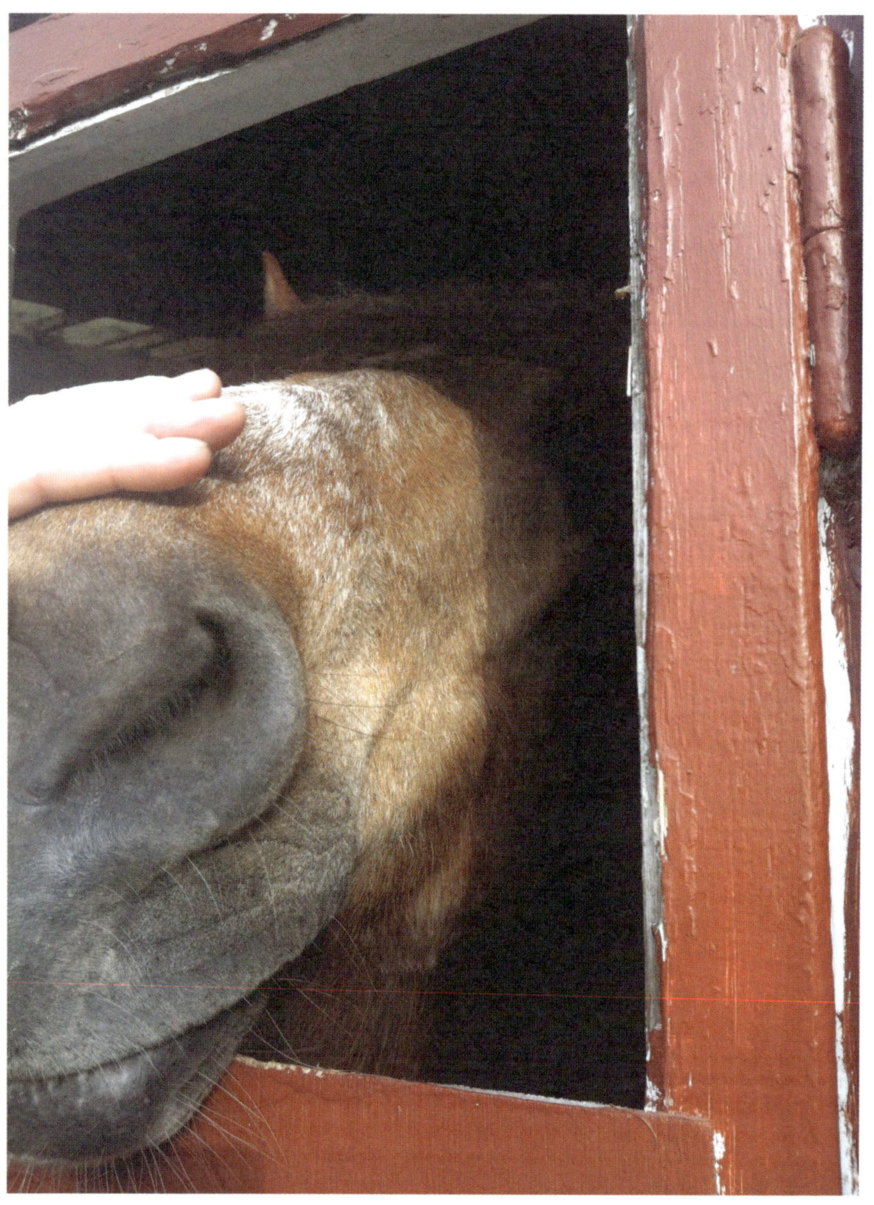

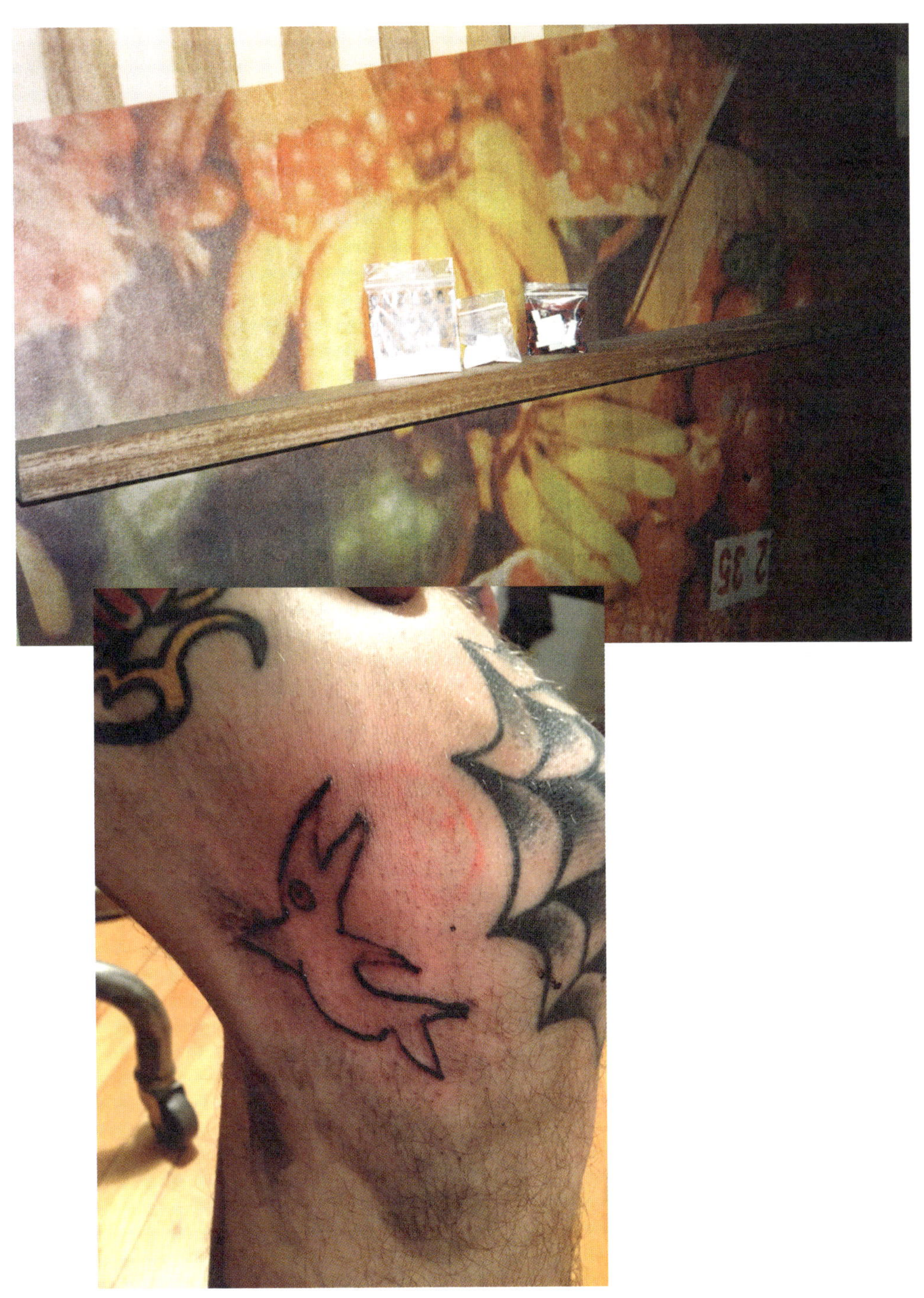

household highs

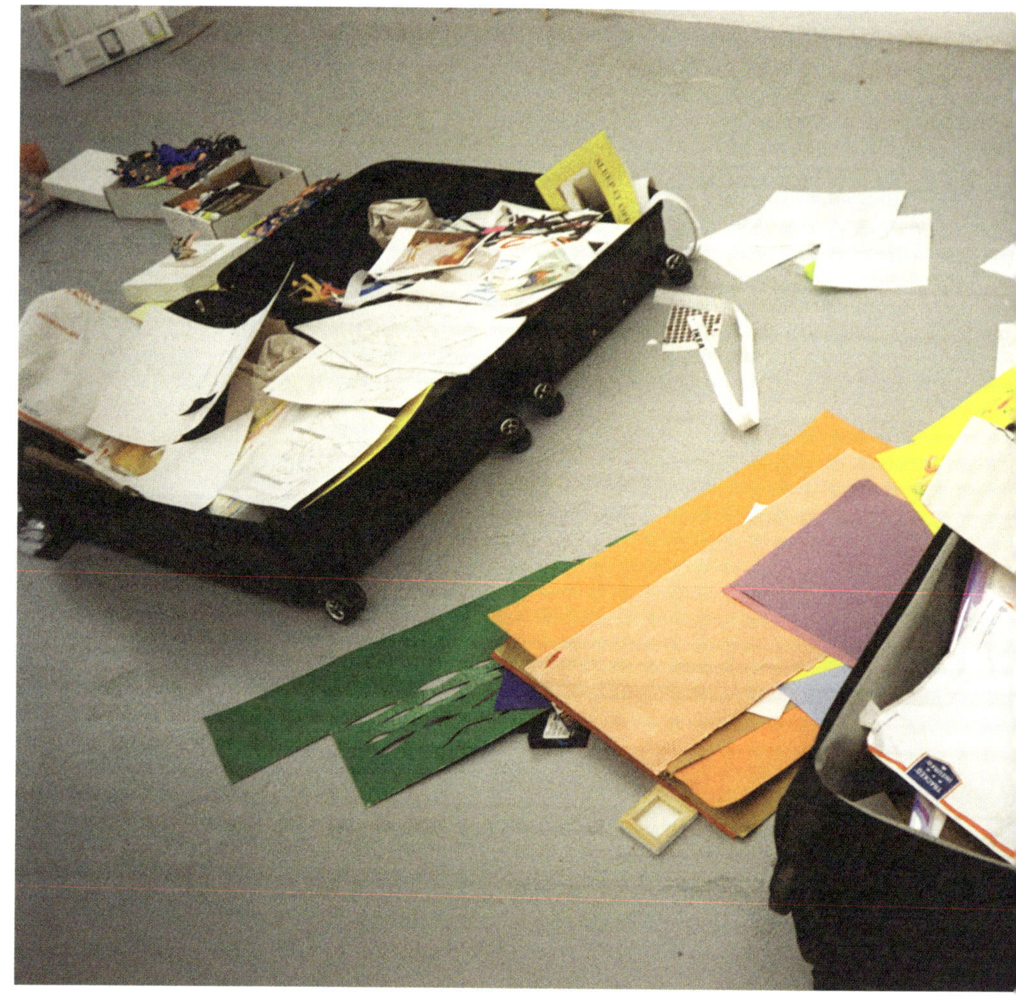

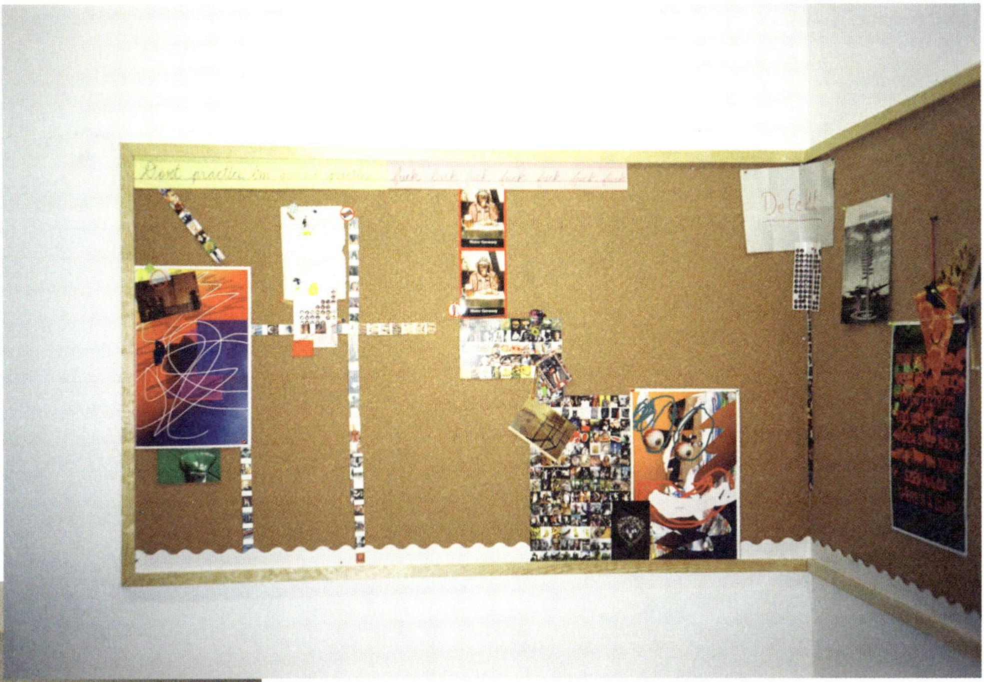

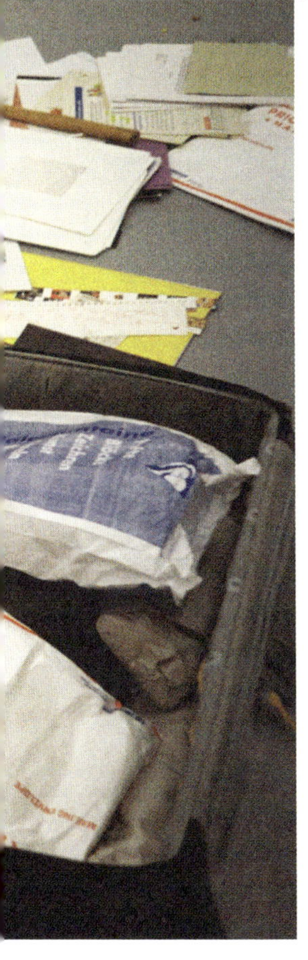

cologne, 2017

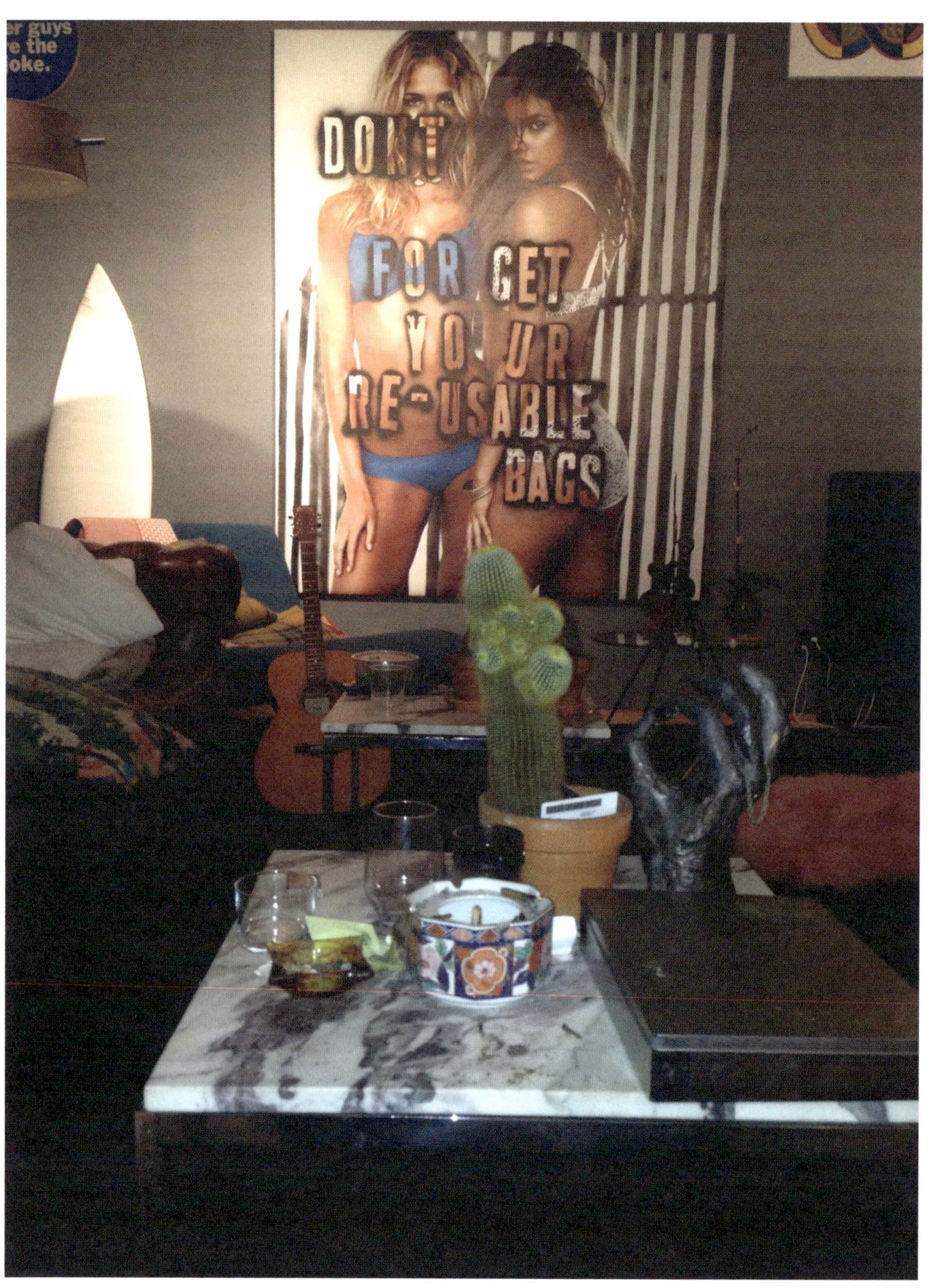
DONT
FOR GET
YOUR
RE-USABLE
BAGS

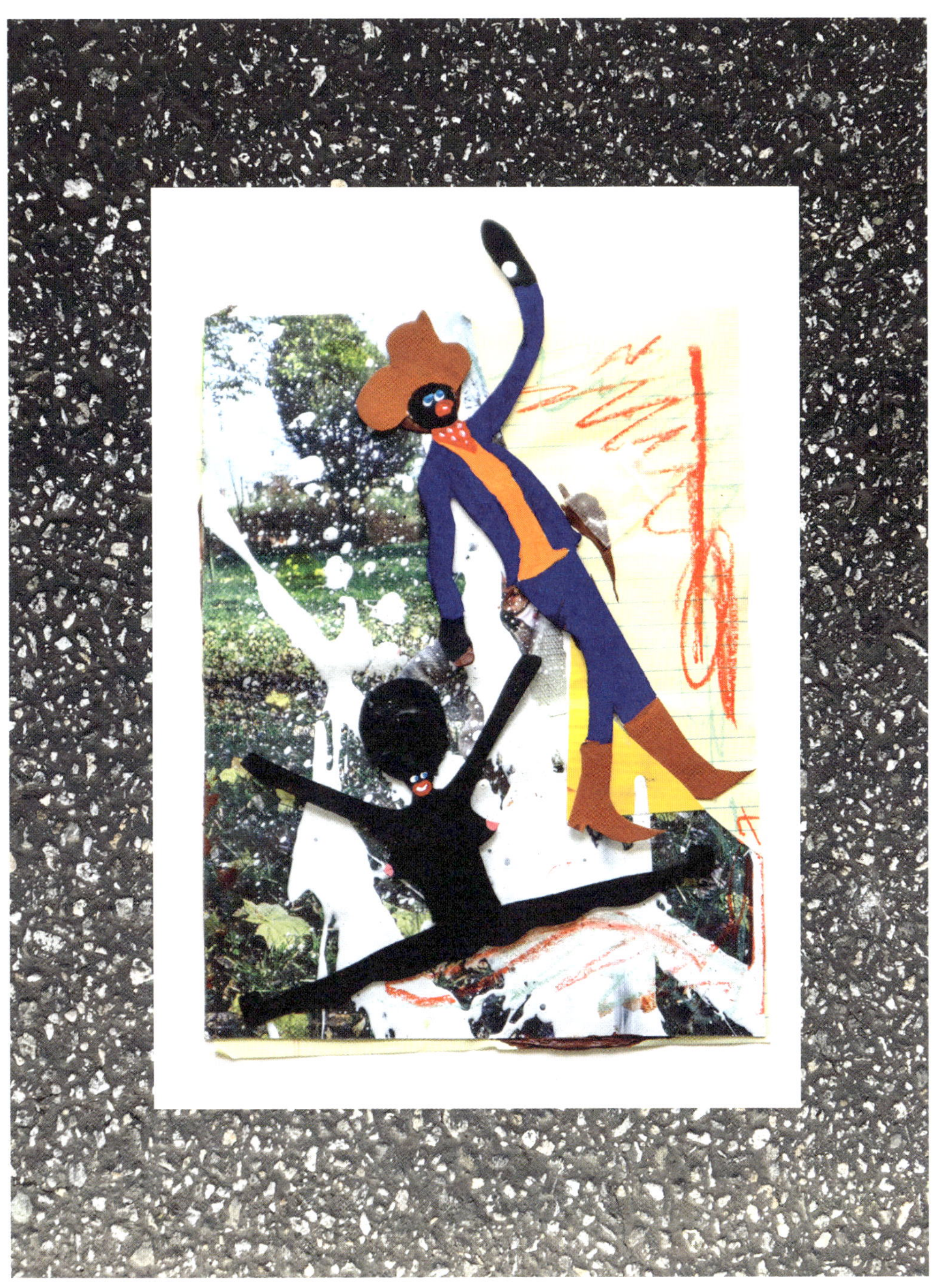

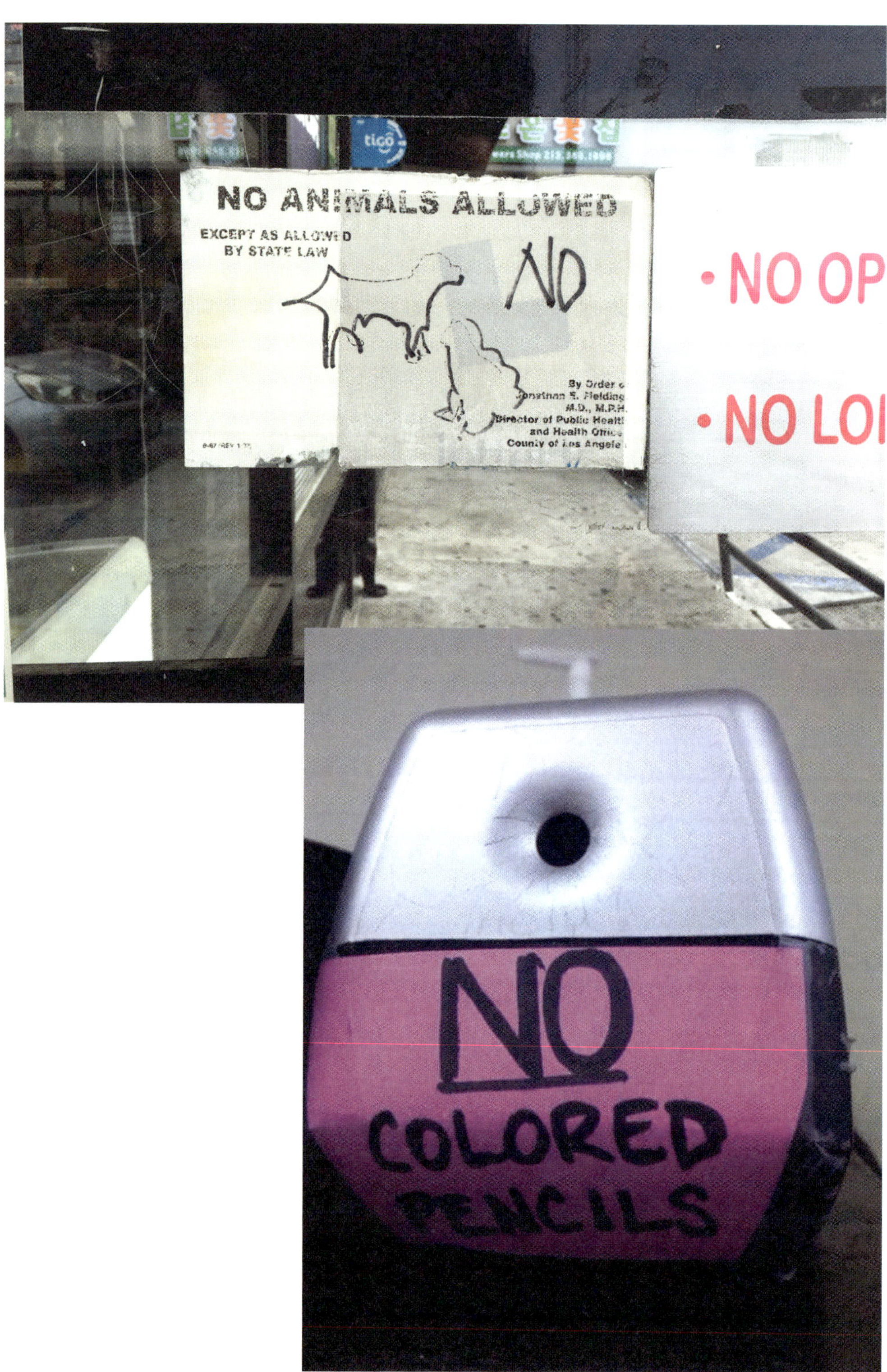
NO ANIMALS ALLOWED
EXCEPT AS ALLOWED
BY STATE LAW
NO
NO
COLORED
PENCILS

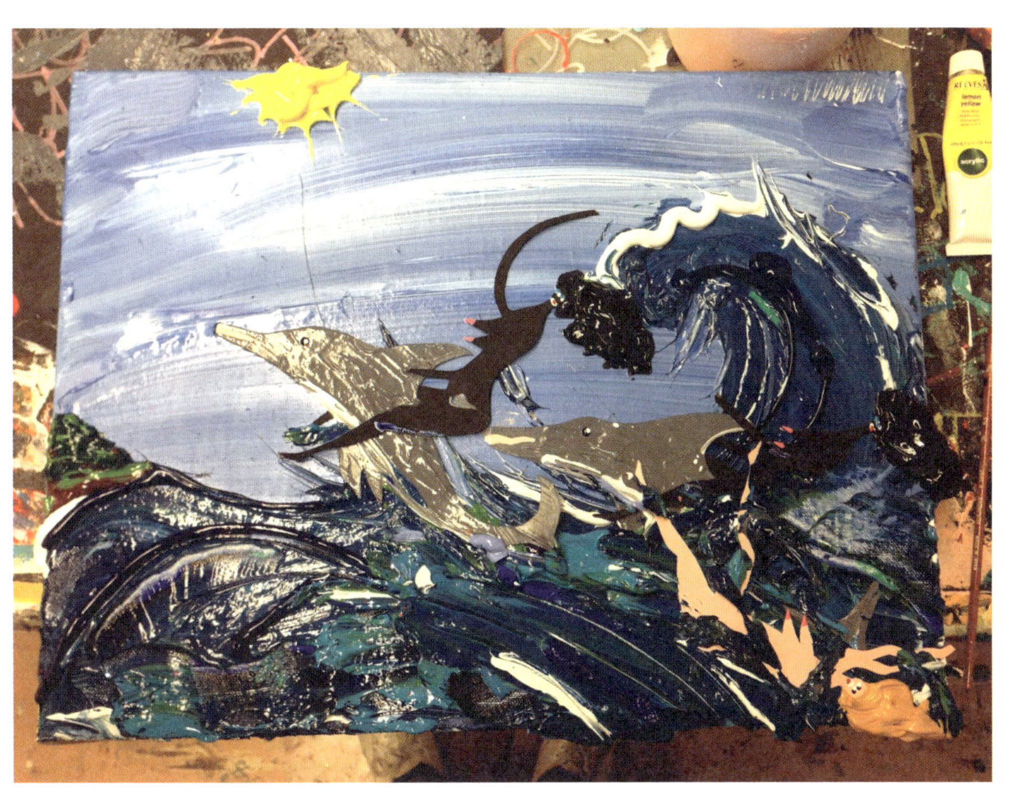

proposed cover for "island of the blue dolphins"

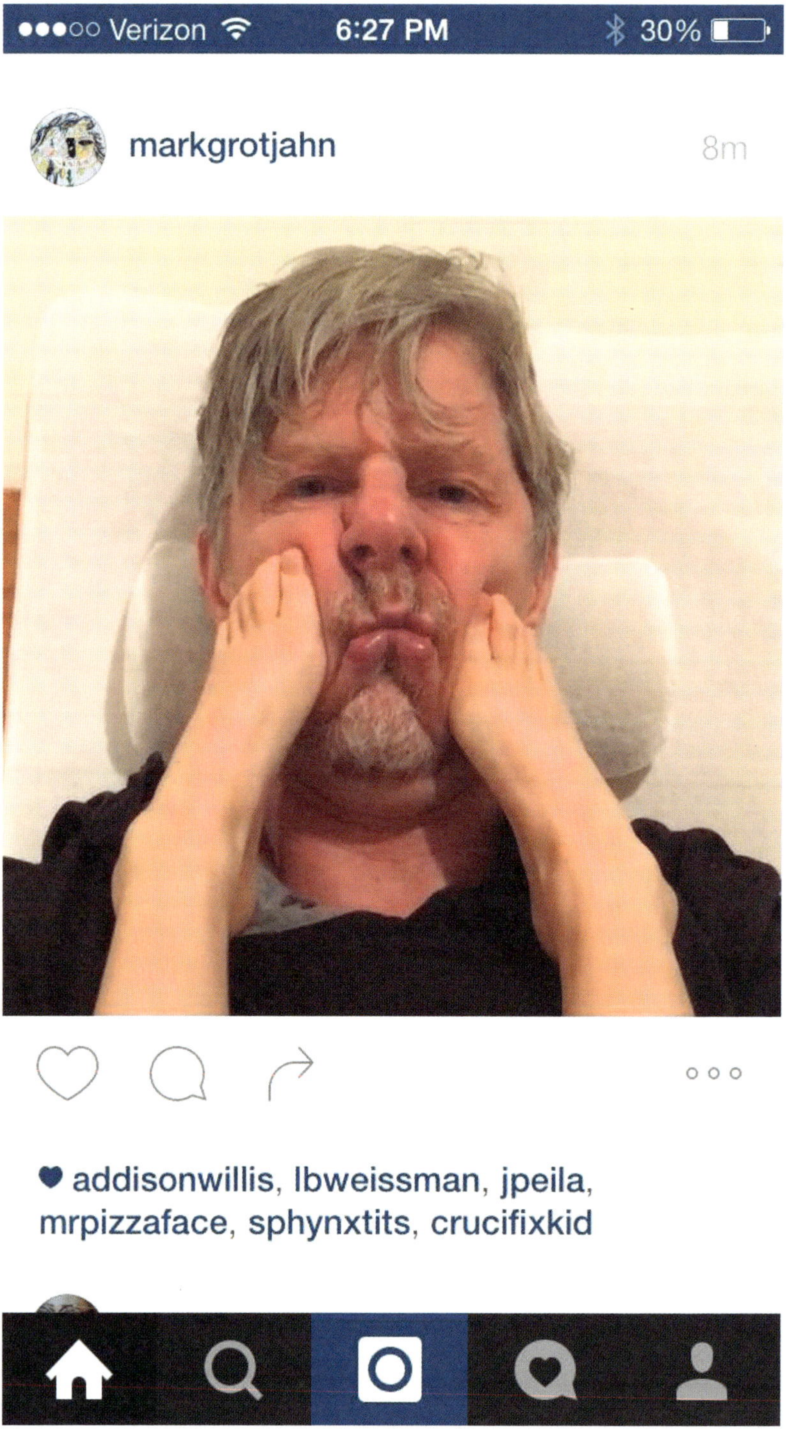

●●●○○ Verizon 6:27 PM 30%

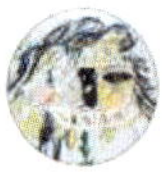

markgrotjahn 8m

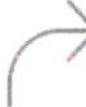

○○○

♥ addisonwillis, lbweissman, jpeila, mrpizzaface, sphynxtits, crucifixkid

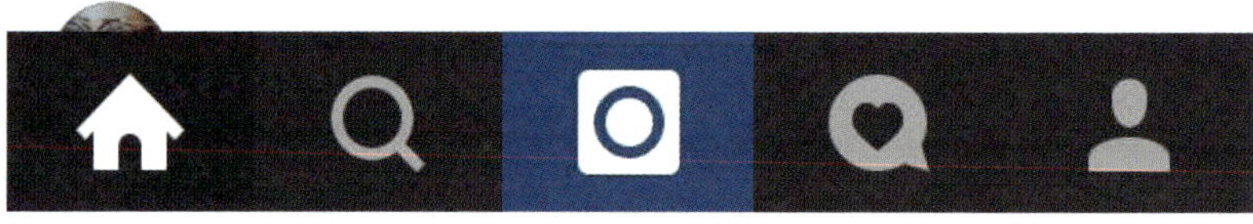

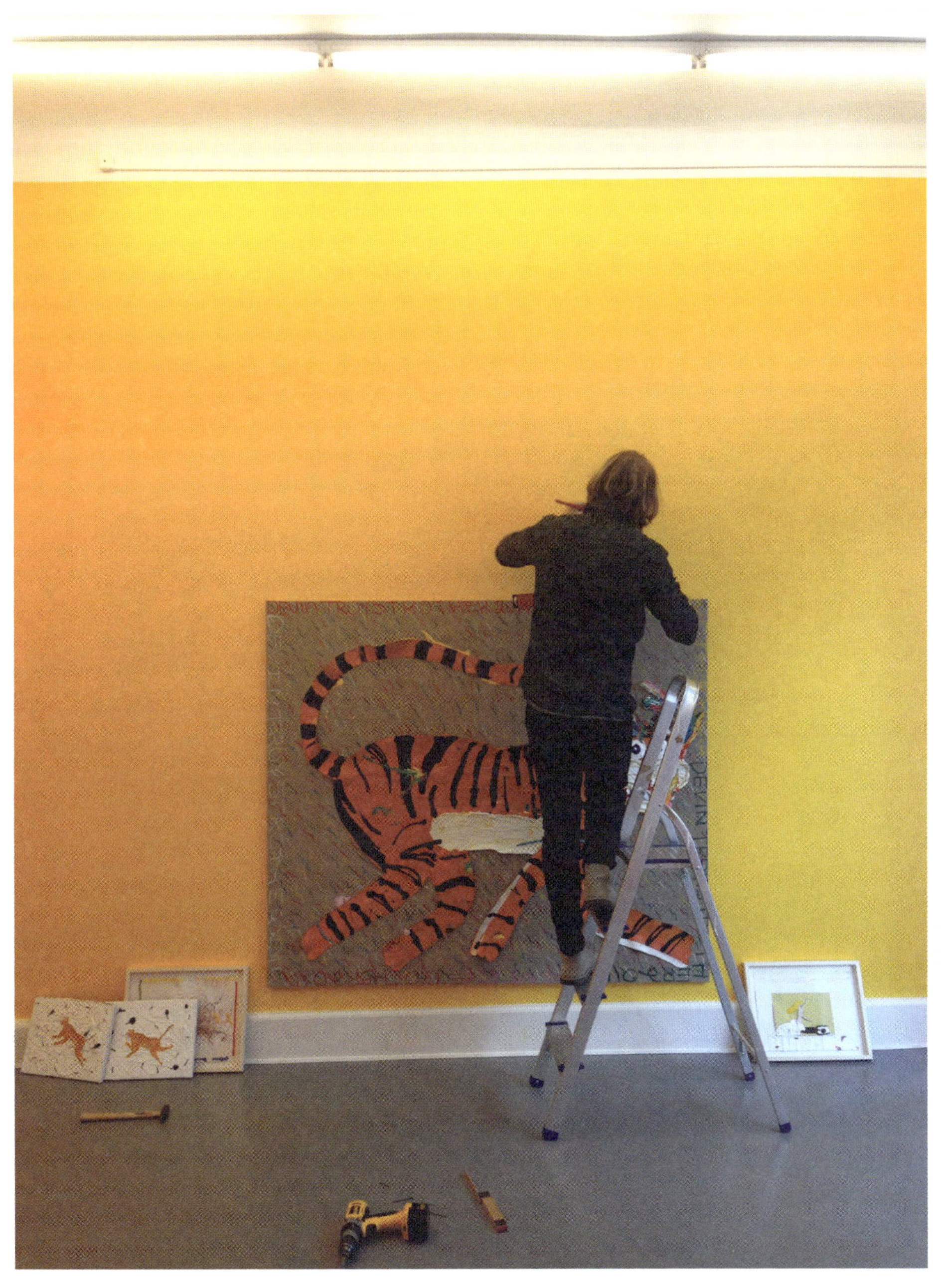

copenhagen, 2014

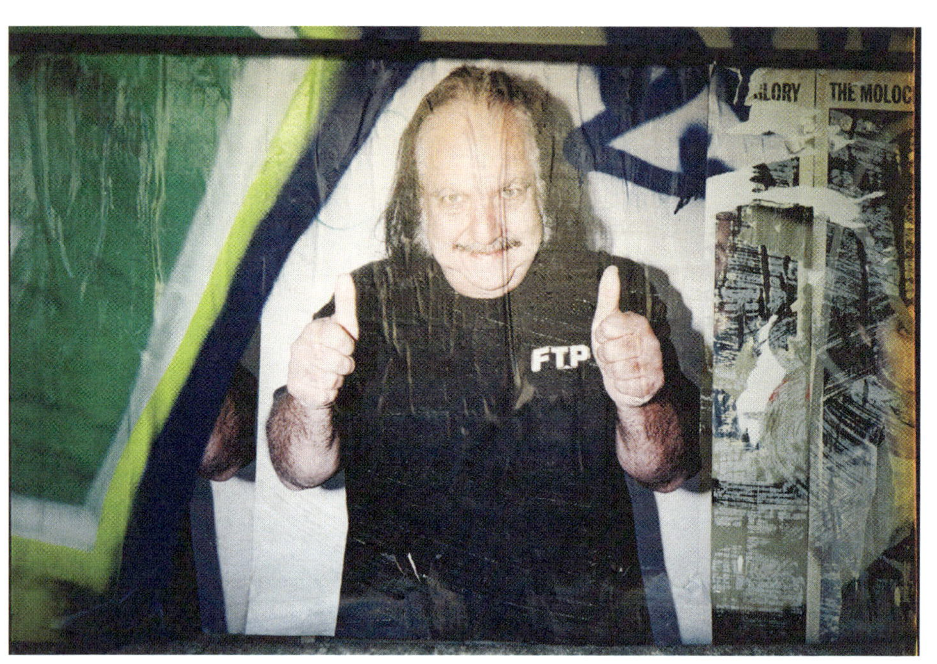
FTP
GLORY
THE MOLOC

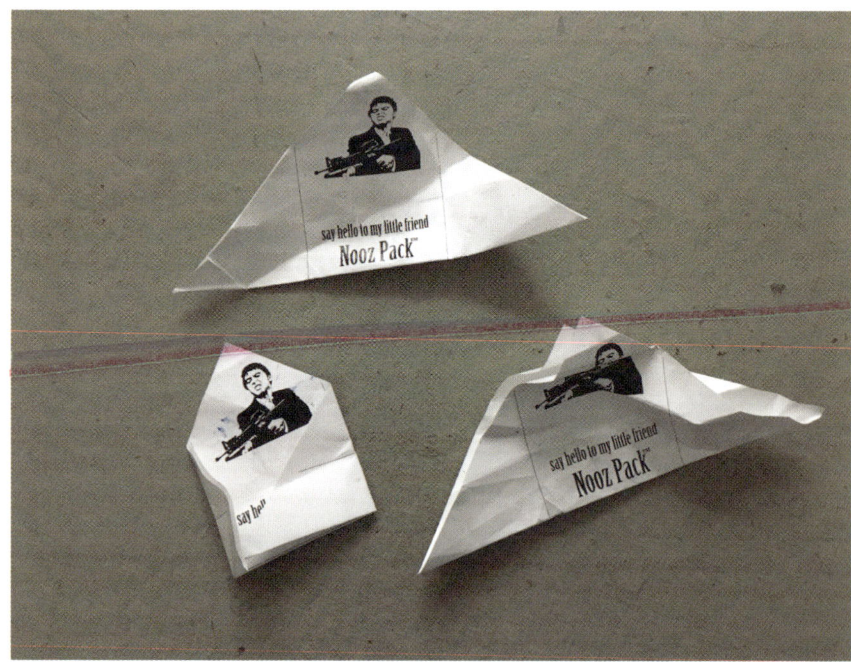
say hello to my little friend
Nooz Pack™
say hello to my little friend
Nooz Pack™
say hel

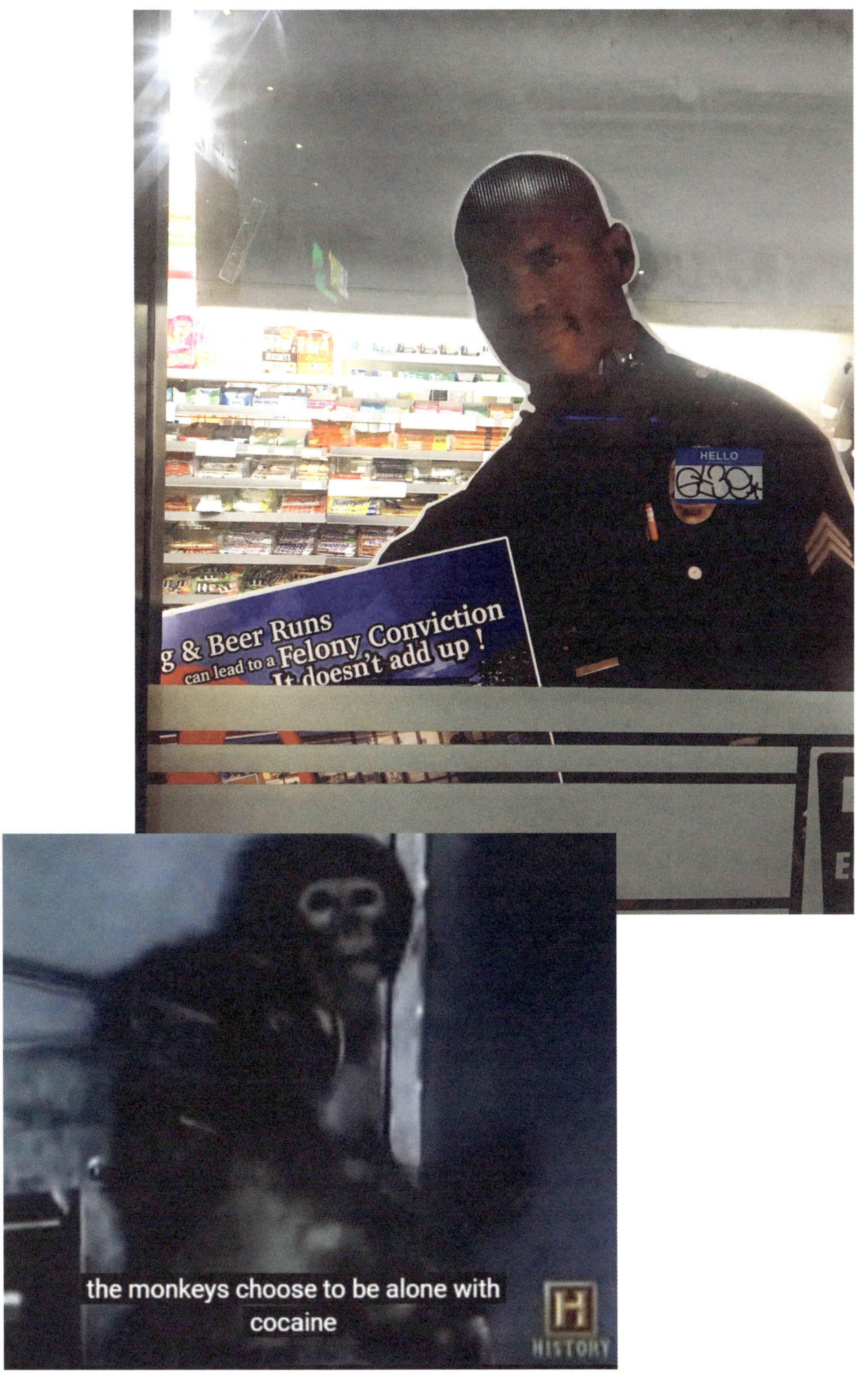
g & Beer Runs
can lead to a Felony Conviction
HELLO
the monkeys choose to be alone with
cocaine
HISTORY

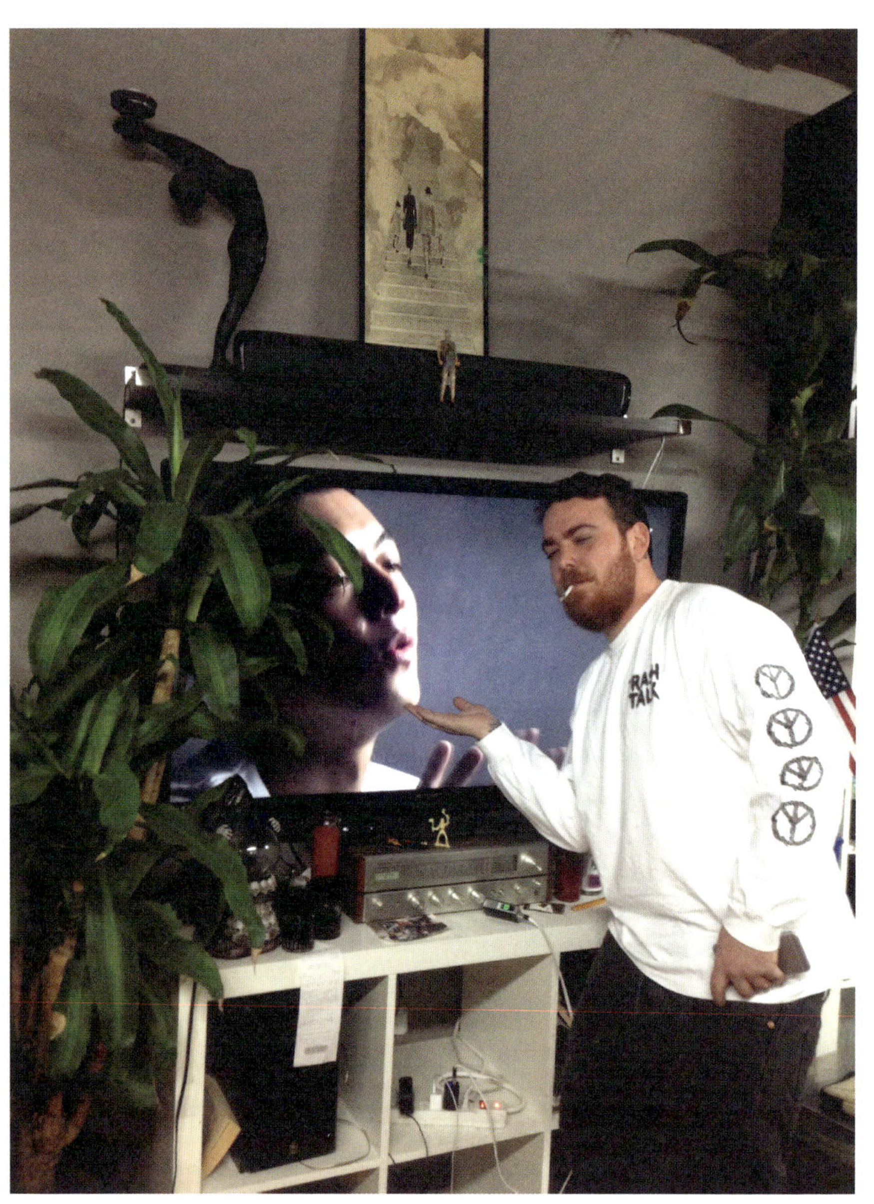

whose mens is this (edison and urbyn)

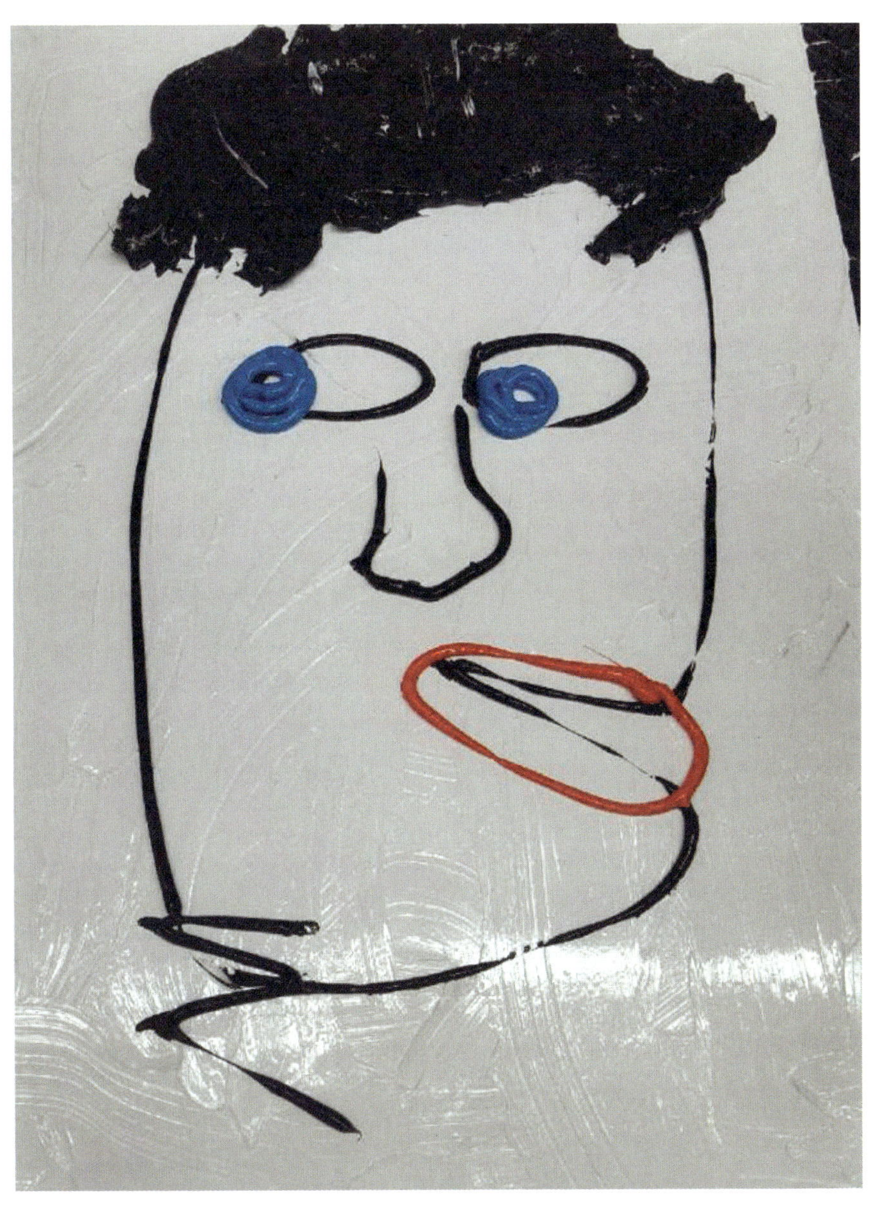

whose mans is this

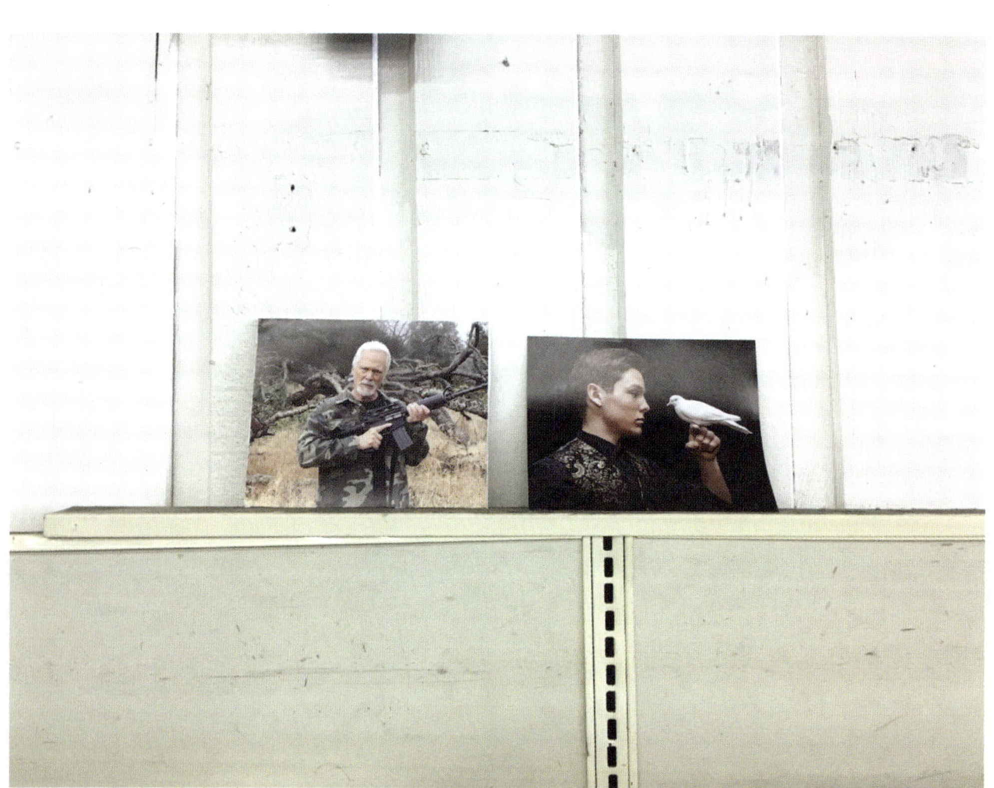

studio 2015 :(
fuck those white girls

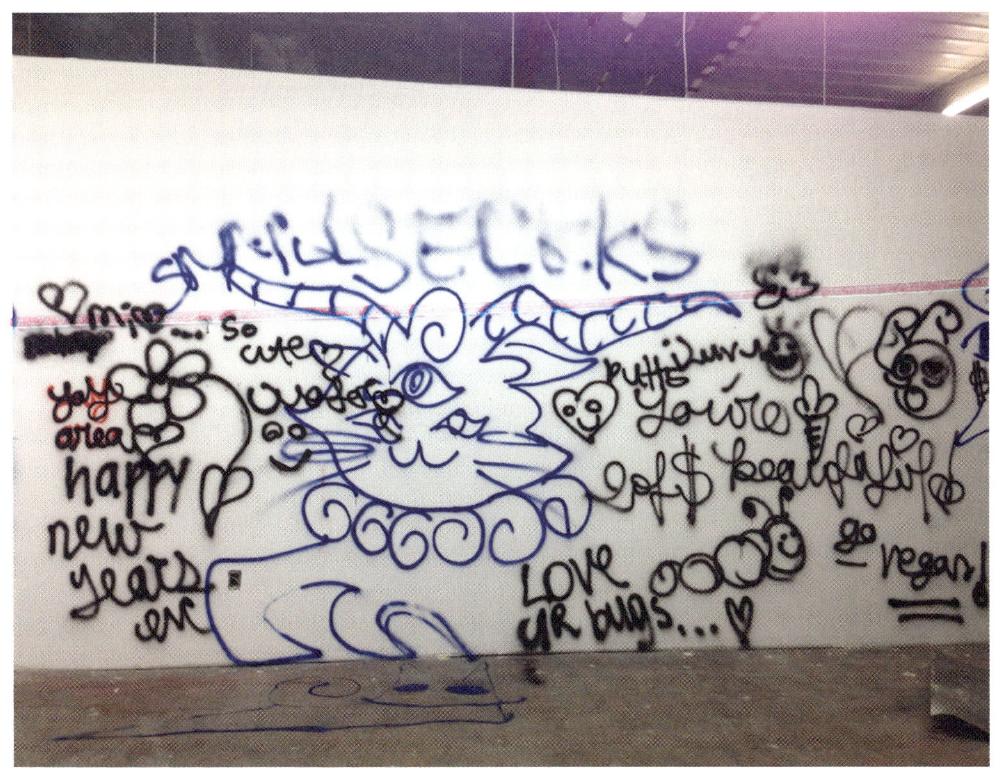

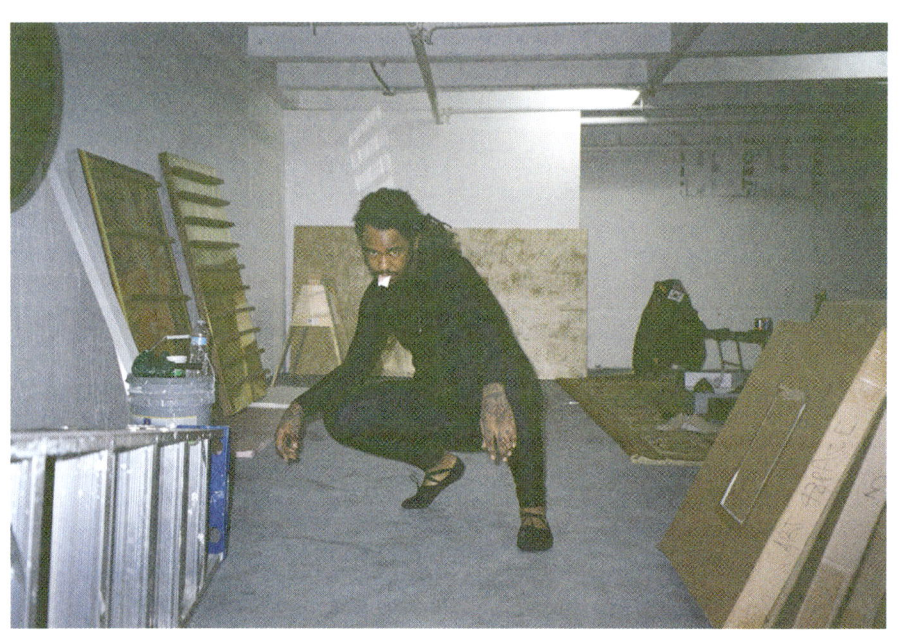

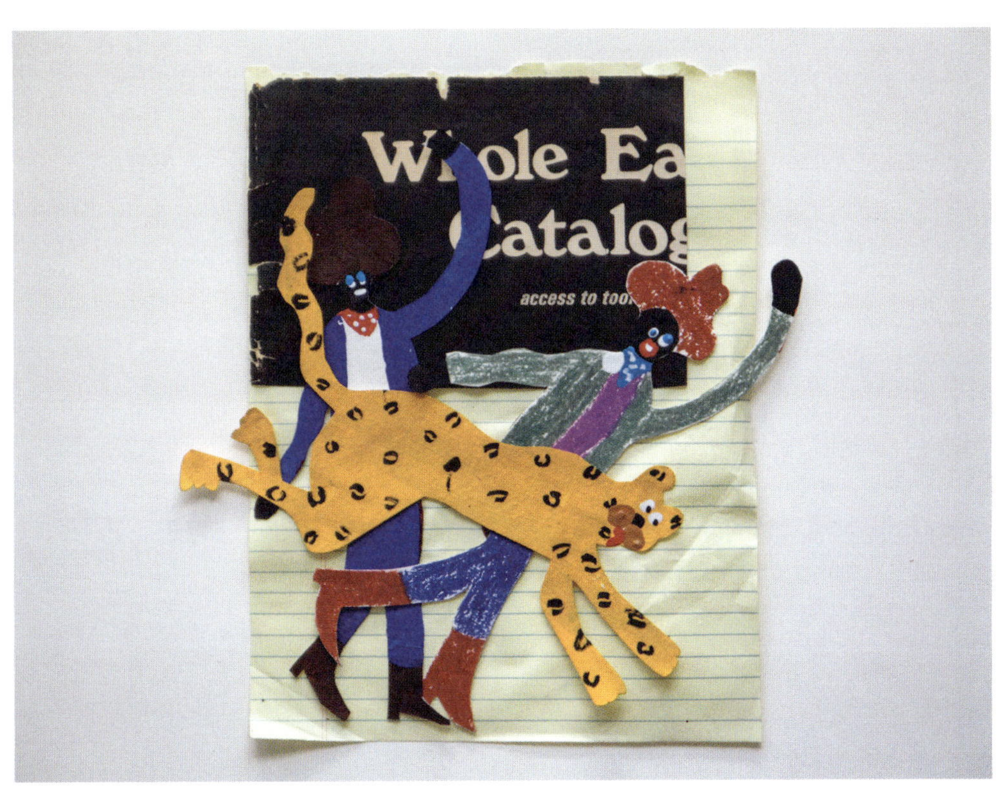
Whole Ea
Catalog
access to too

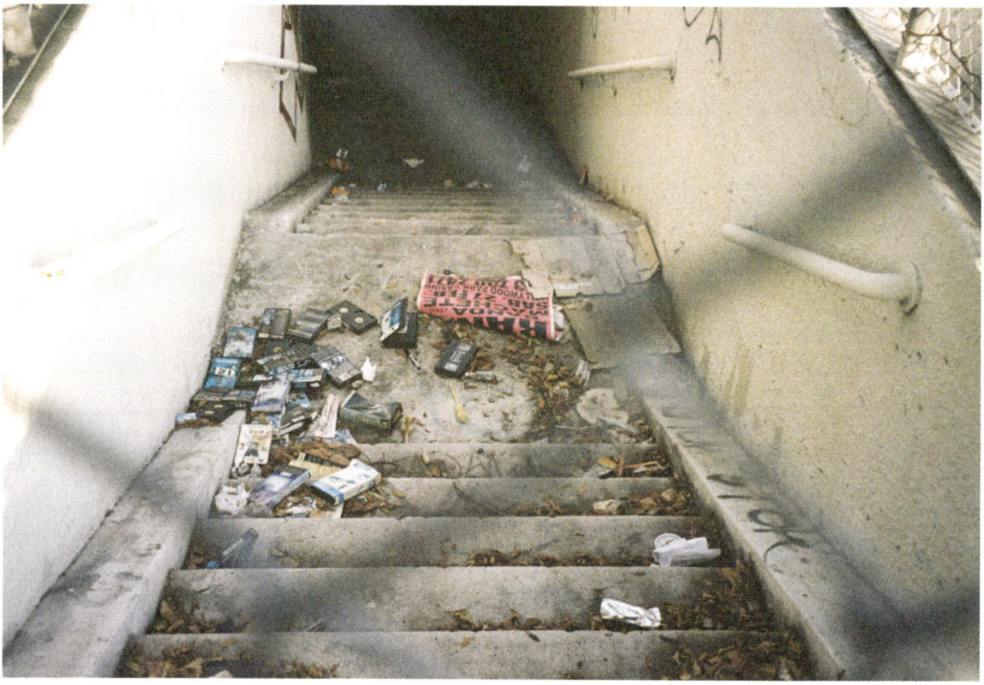

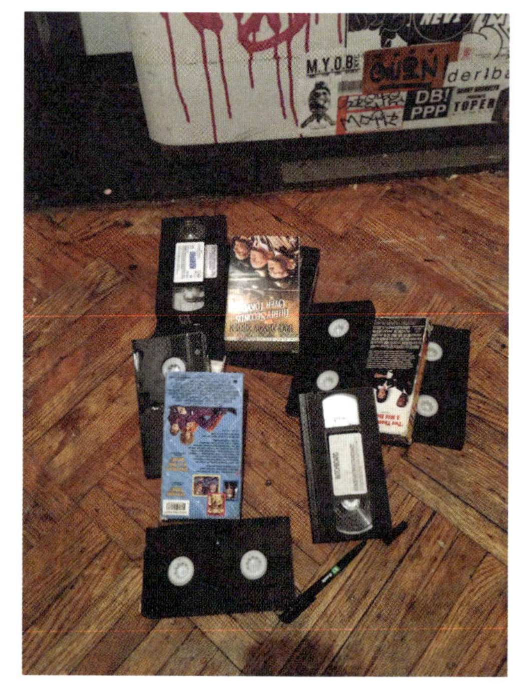
M.Y.O.B
DB!
PPP
TOPER

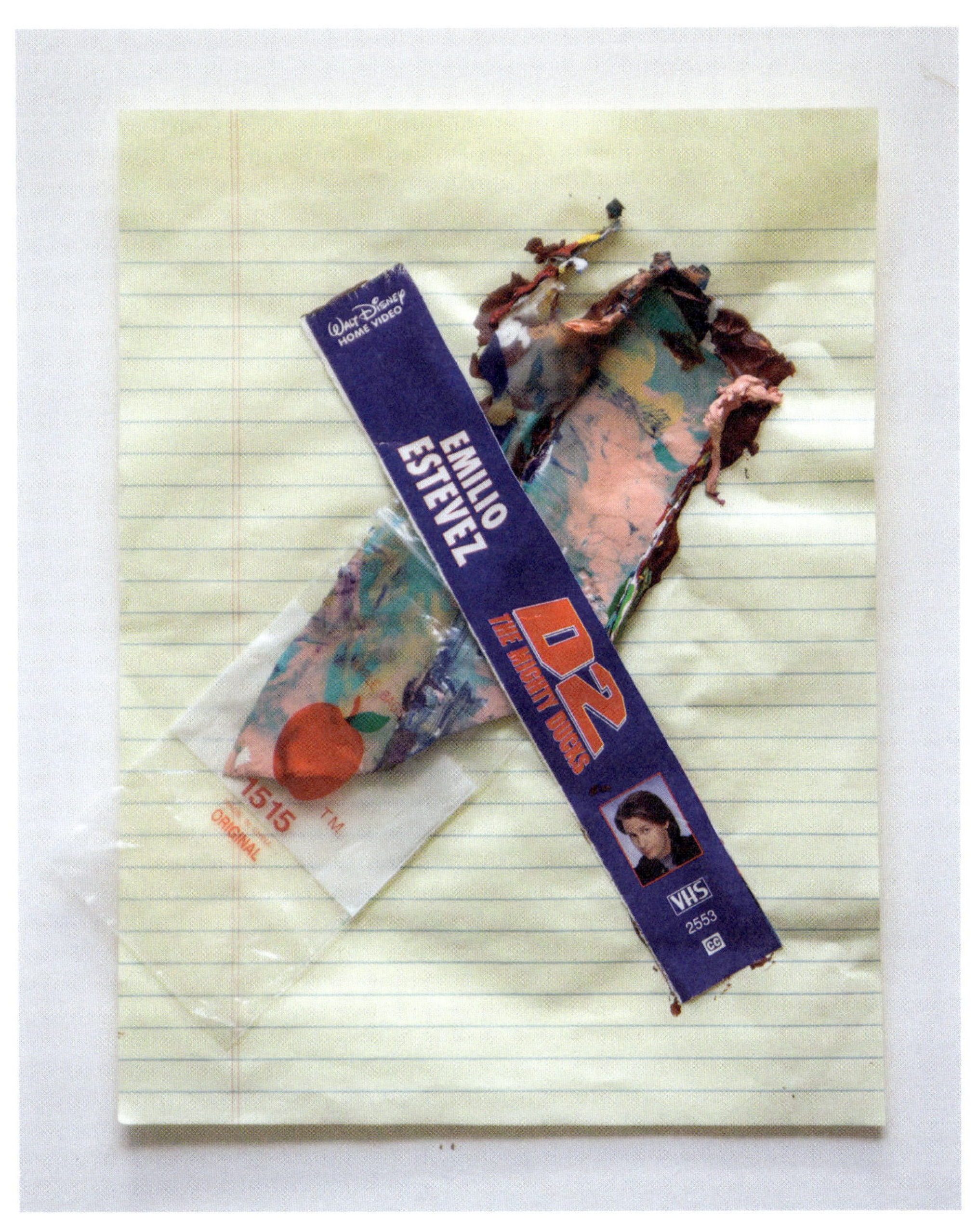

now that's some fine cinema

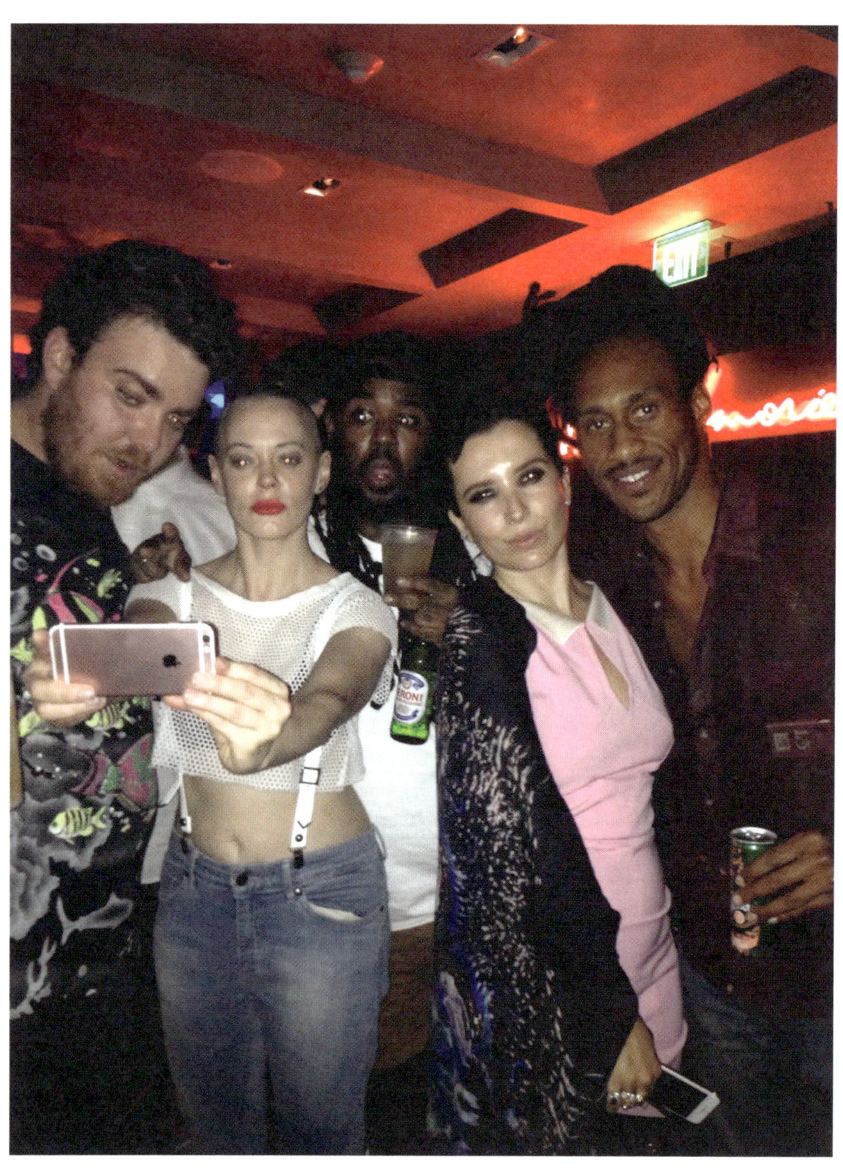

urbyn, rose, devin, aureta, and watts

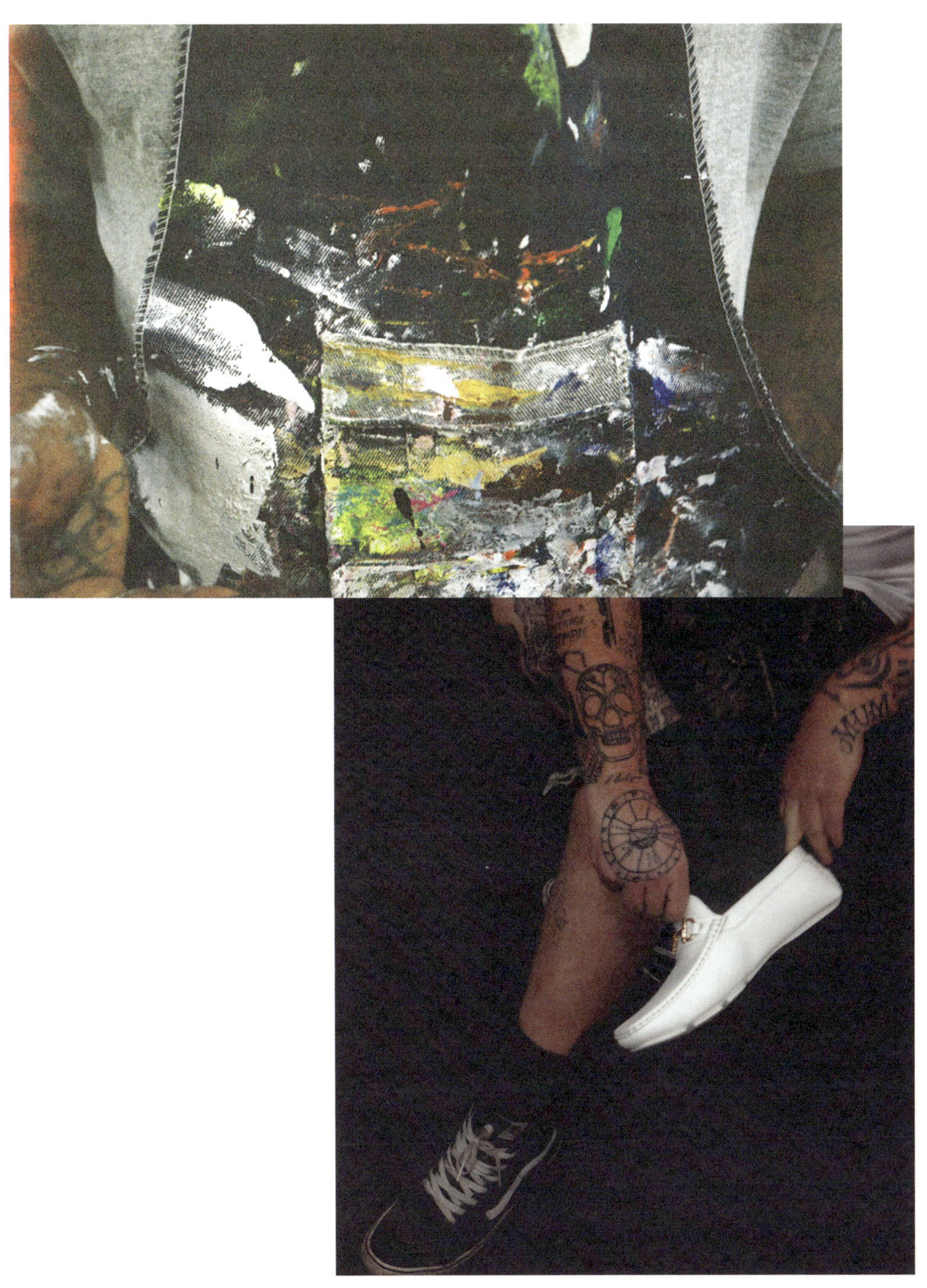

twinkle toes

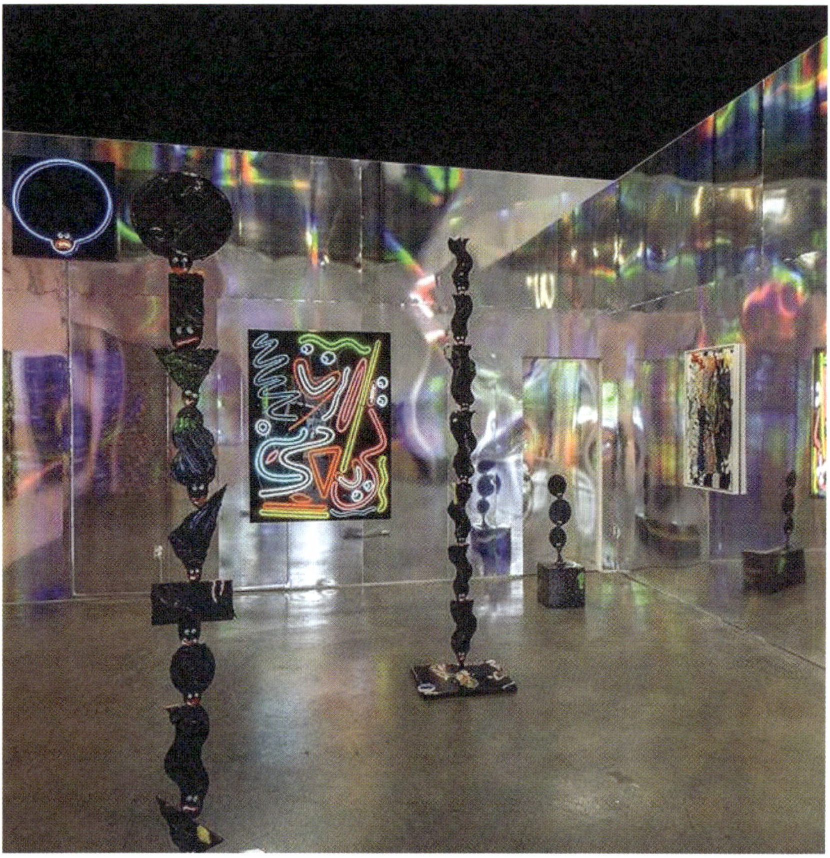

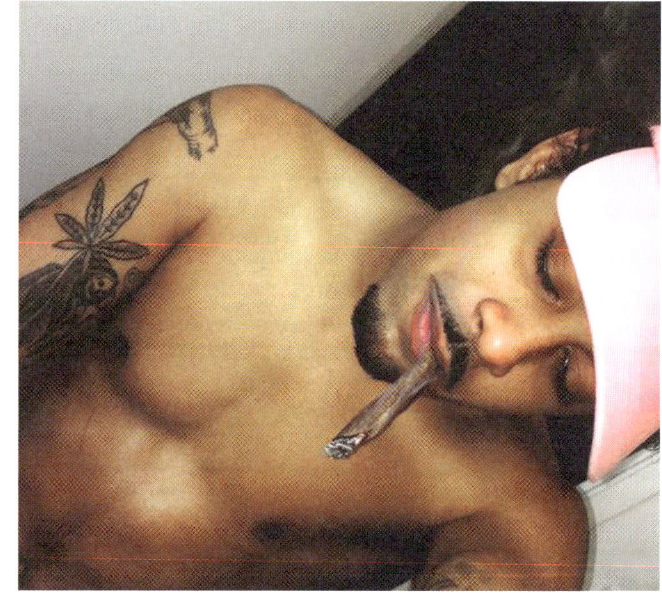

that nigga georgio

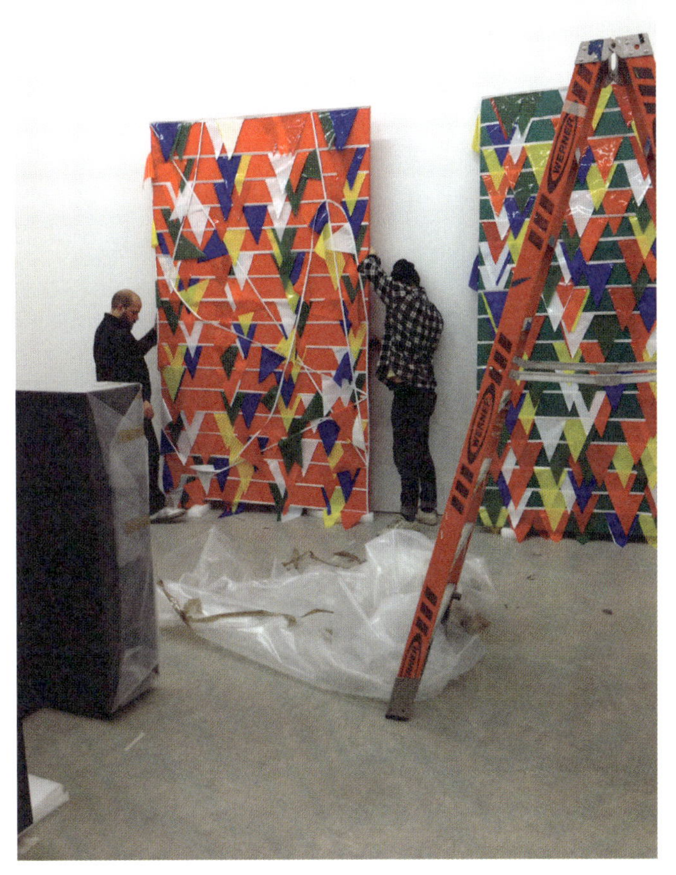

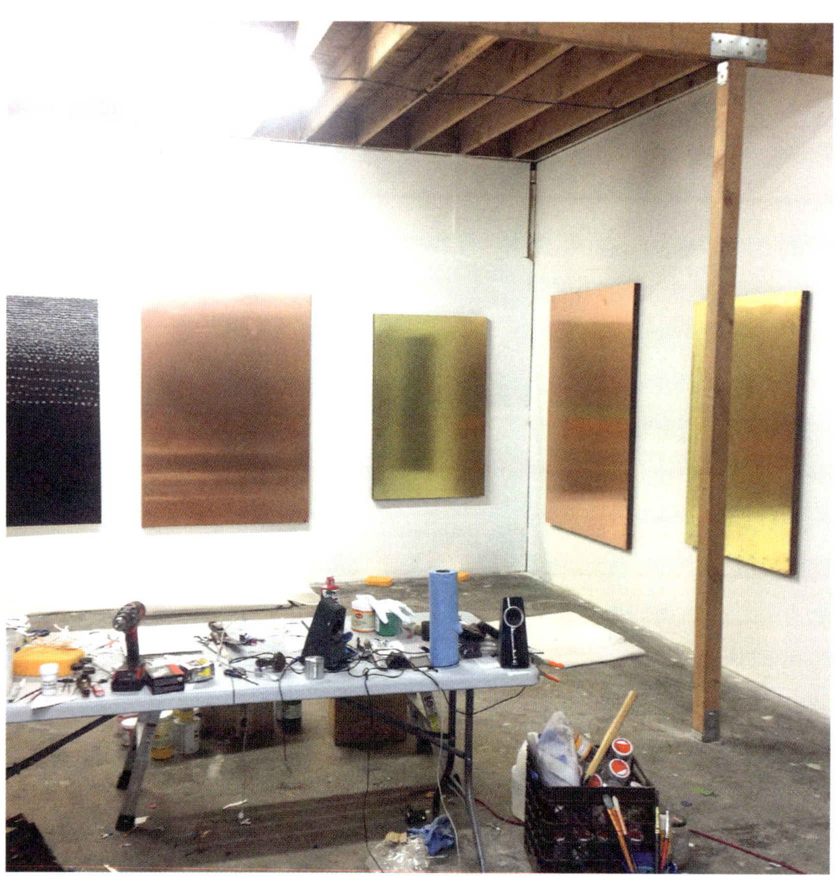

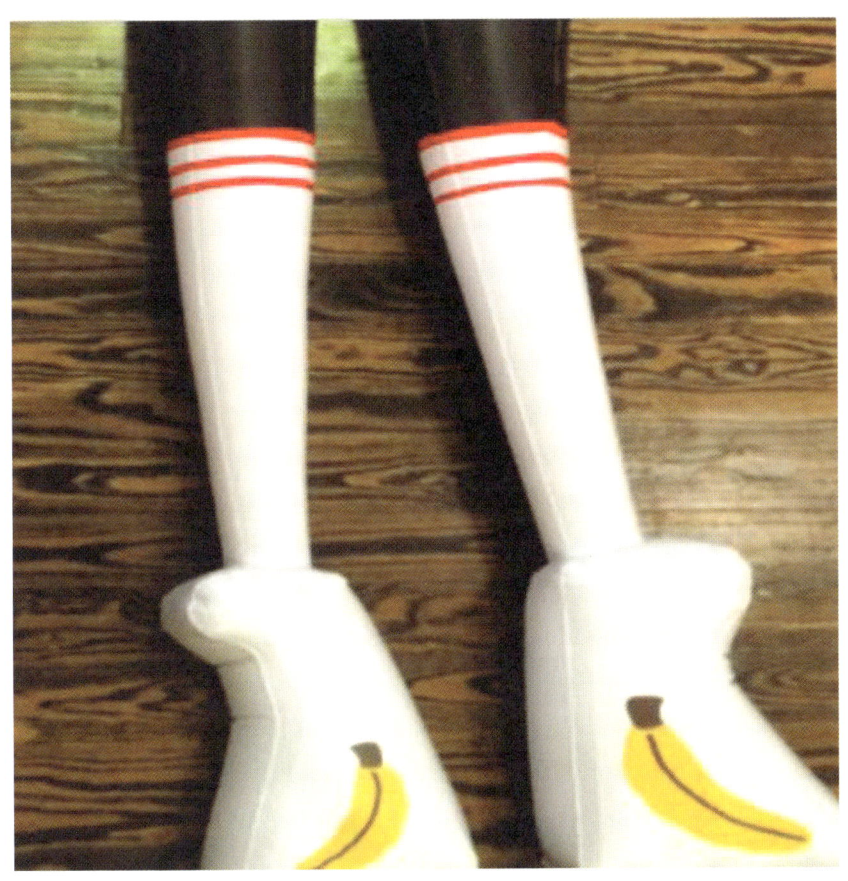

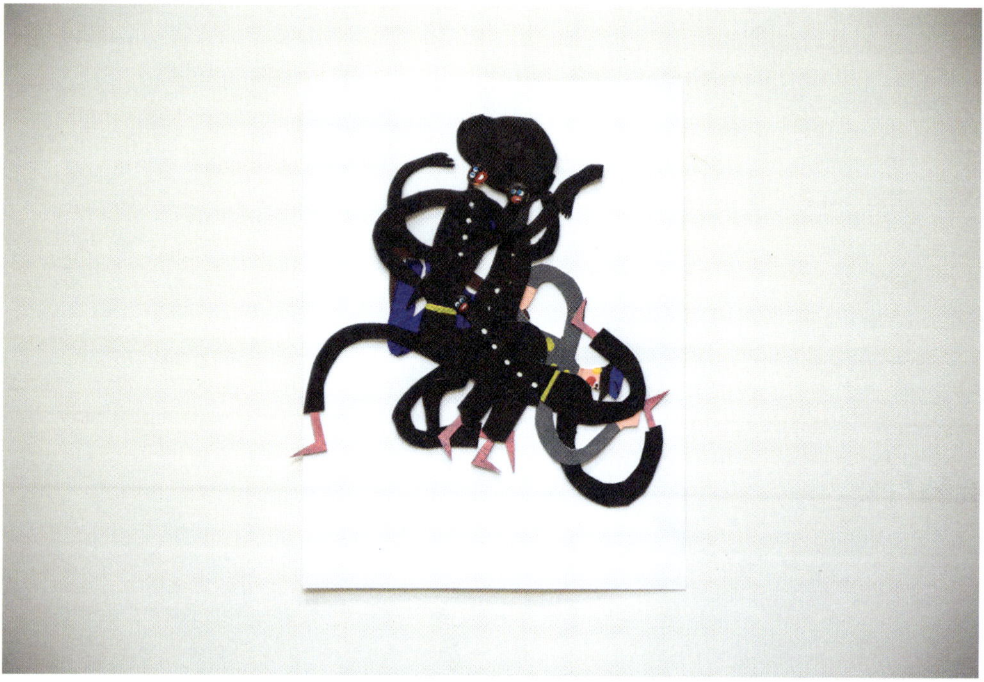

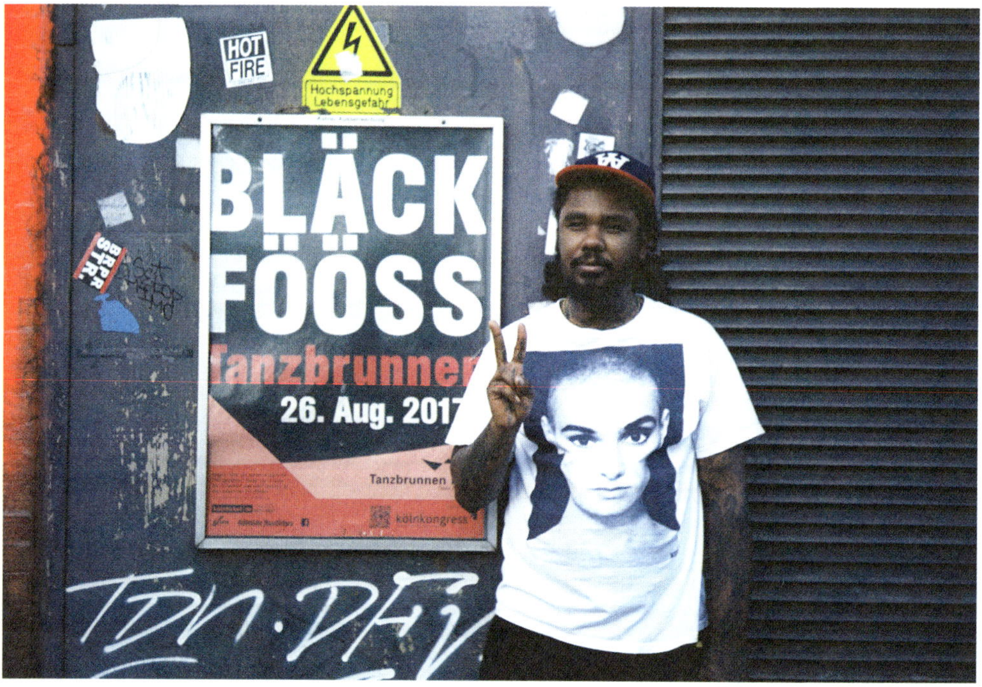

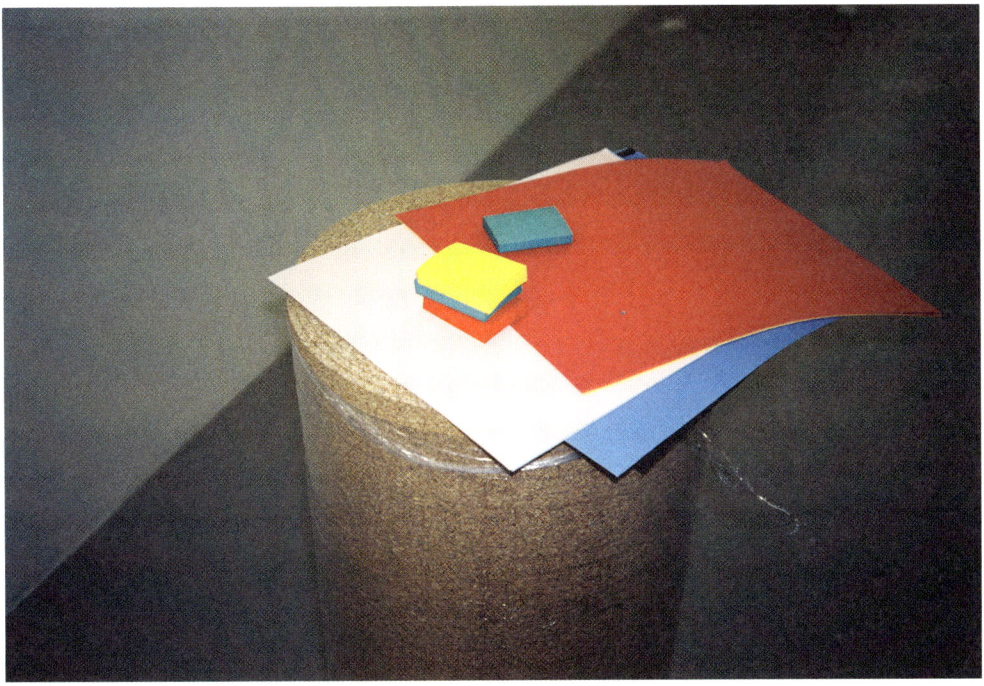

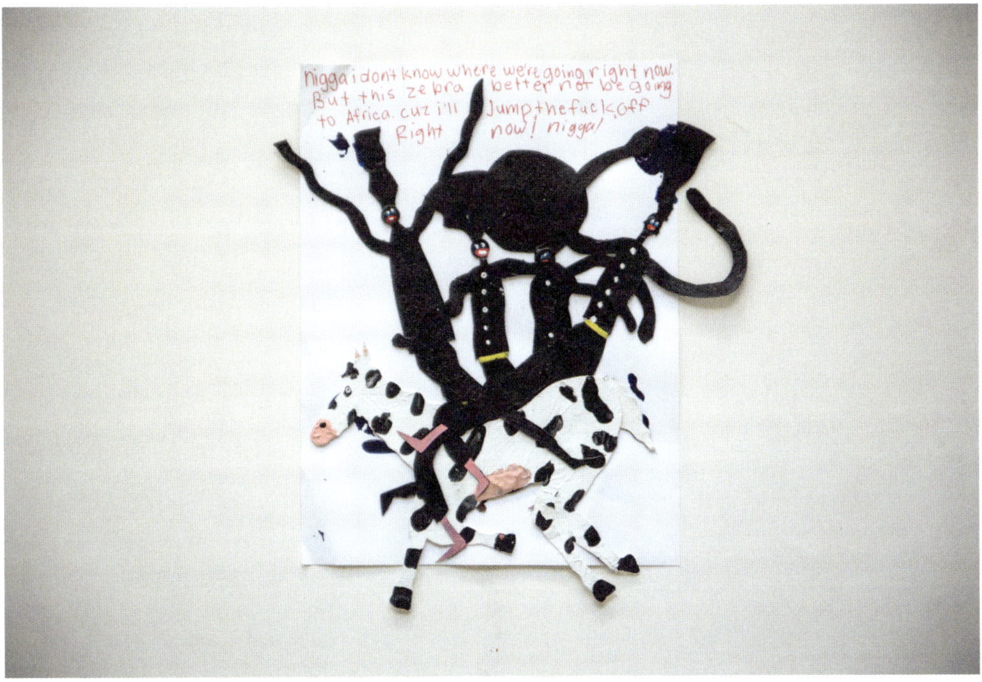
nigga i don't know where we're going right now.
But this zebra better not be going
to Africa. cuz i'll Jump the fuck off
Right now! nigga!

yuri at andy milonakis' house, 2013

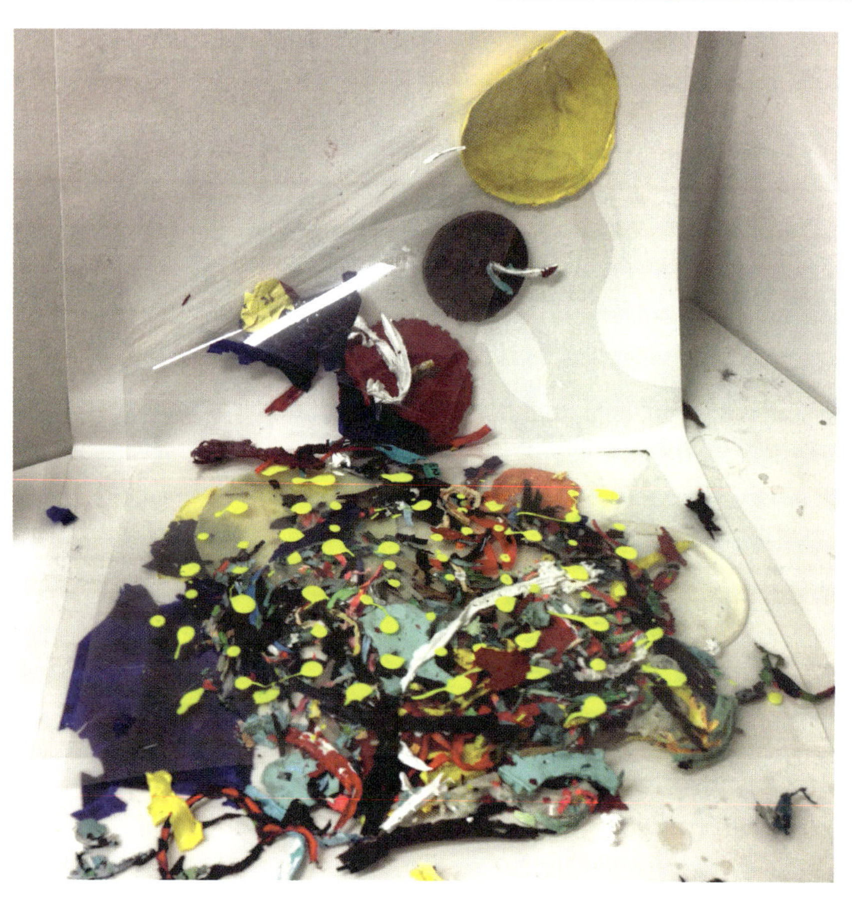

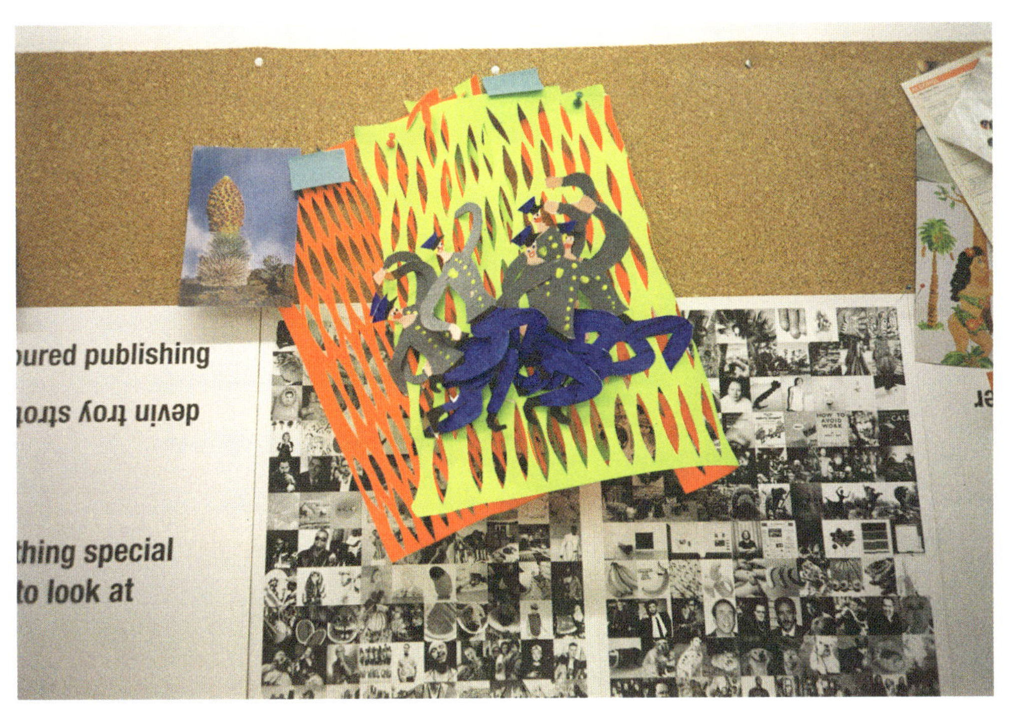

cologne, 2017

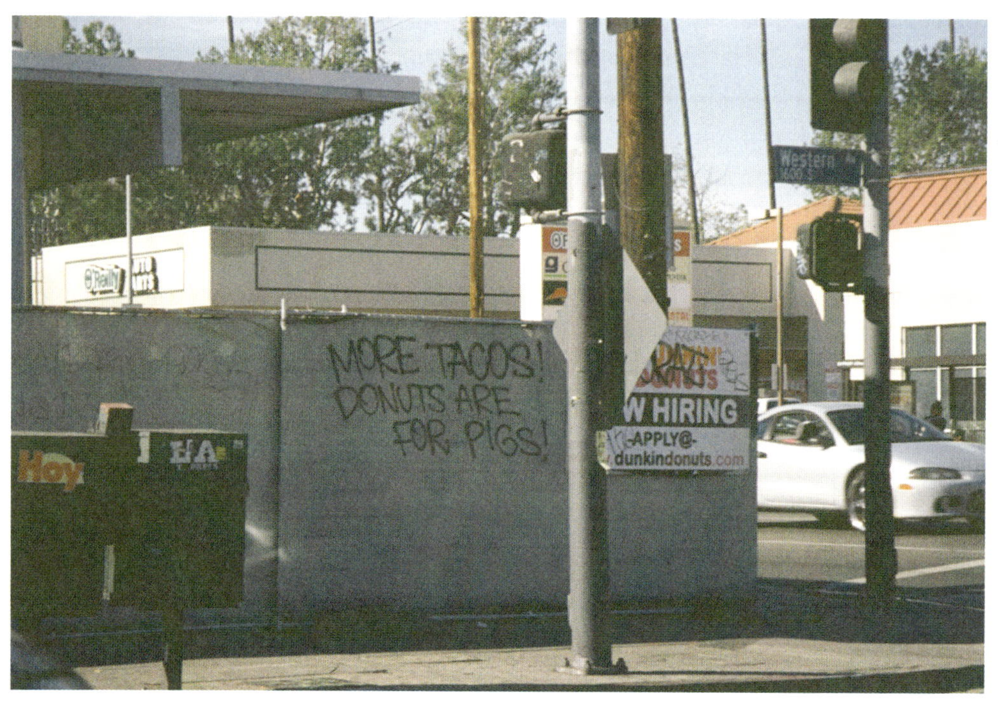
MORE TACOS!
DONUTS ARE
FOR PIGS!
W HIRING
-APPLY@-
dunkindonuts.com
Western
Hoy

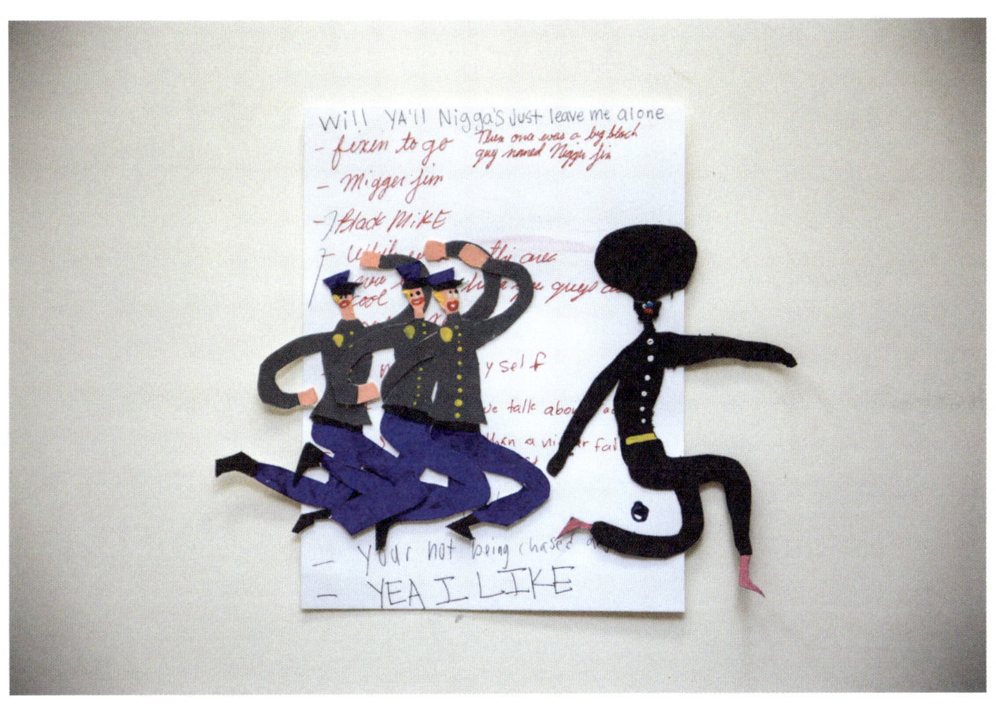
Will YA'll Nigga's Just leave me alone
- fixen to go
- Nigger Jim
- Black MIKE
- YEA I LIKE

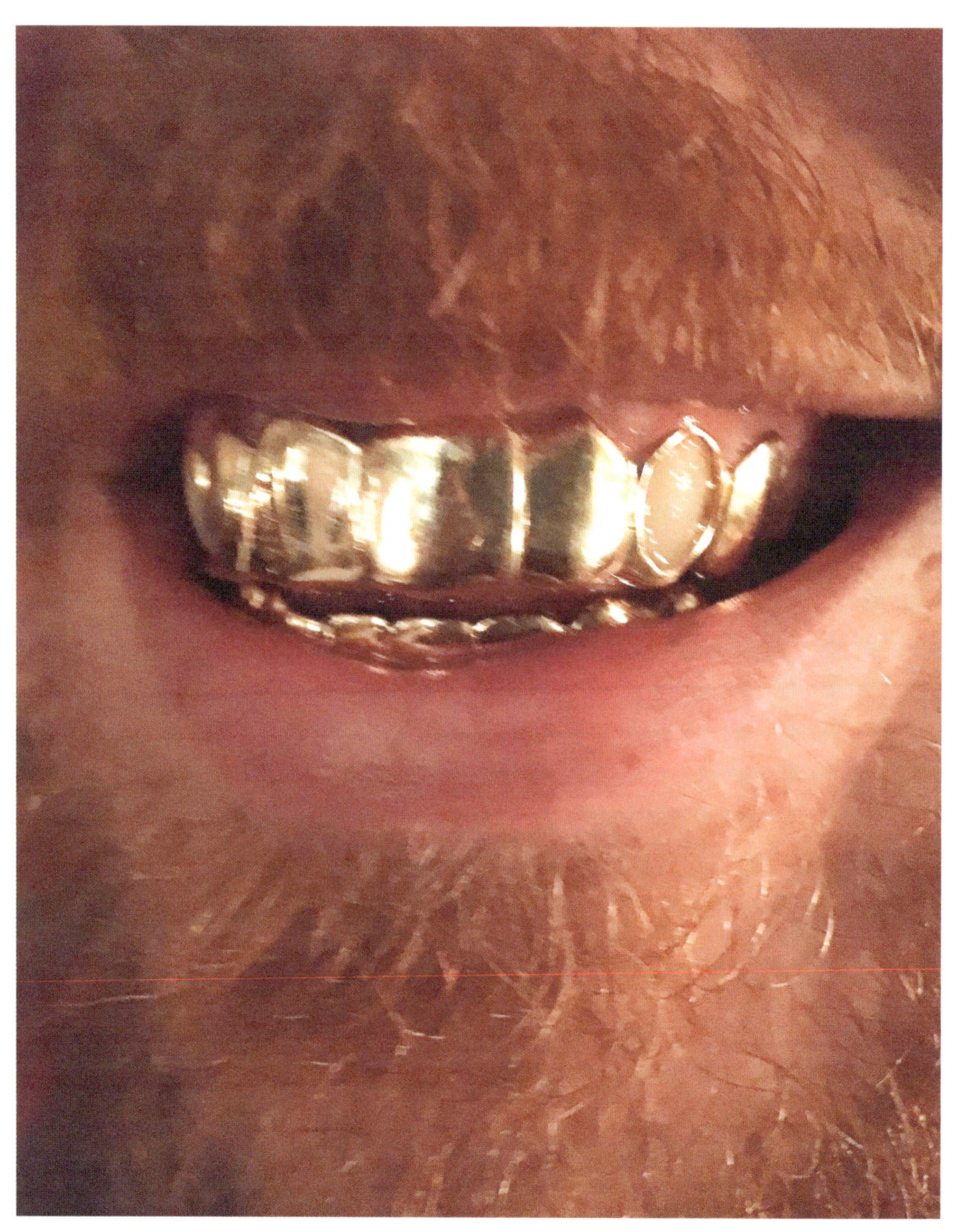

fuck australians (except this one)

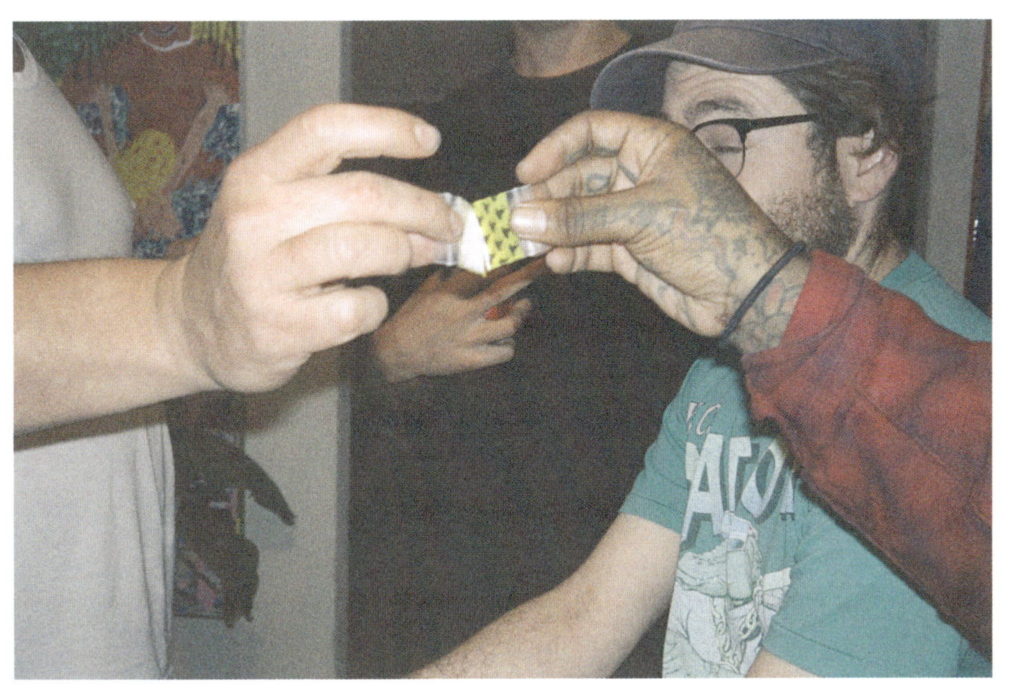

cheers!

A Mistake Is A Beautiful Thing

Photographs by Devin Troy Strother &
Yuri Ogita

Published by Printed Matter, Inc. with
Coloured Publishing

2018

Edition of 500 copies

Printed by KOPA, Lithuania

Printed Matter, Inc.
231 11th Avenue
New York, NY 10001
www.printedmatter.org

ISBN : 978-0-89439-096-8

Printed Matter's publishing program is generously supported by The Andy Warhol Foundation for the Visual Arts and the New York City Department of Cultural Affairs

Printed Matter, Inc.

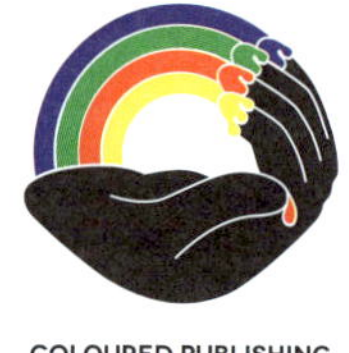

COLOURED PUBLISHING

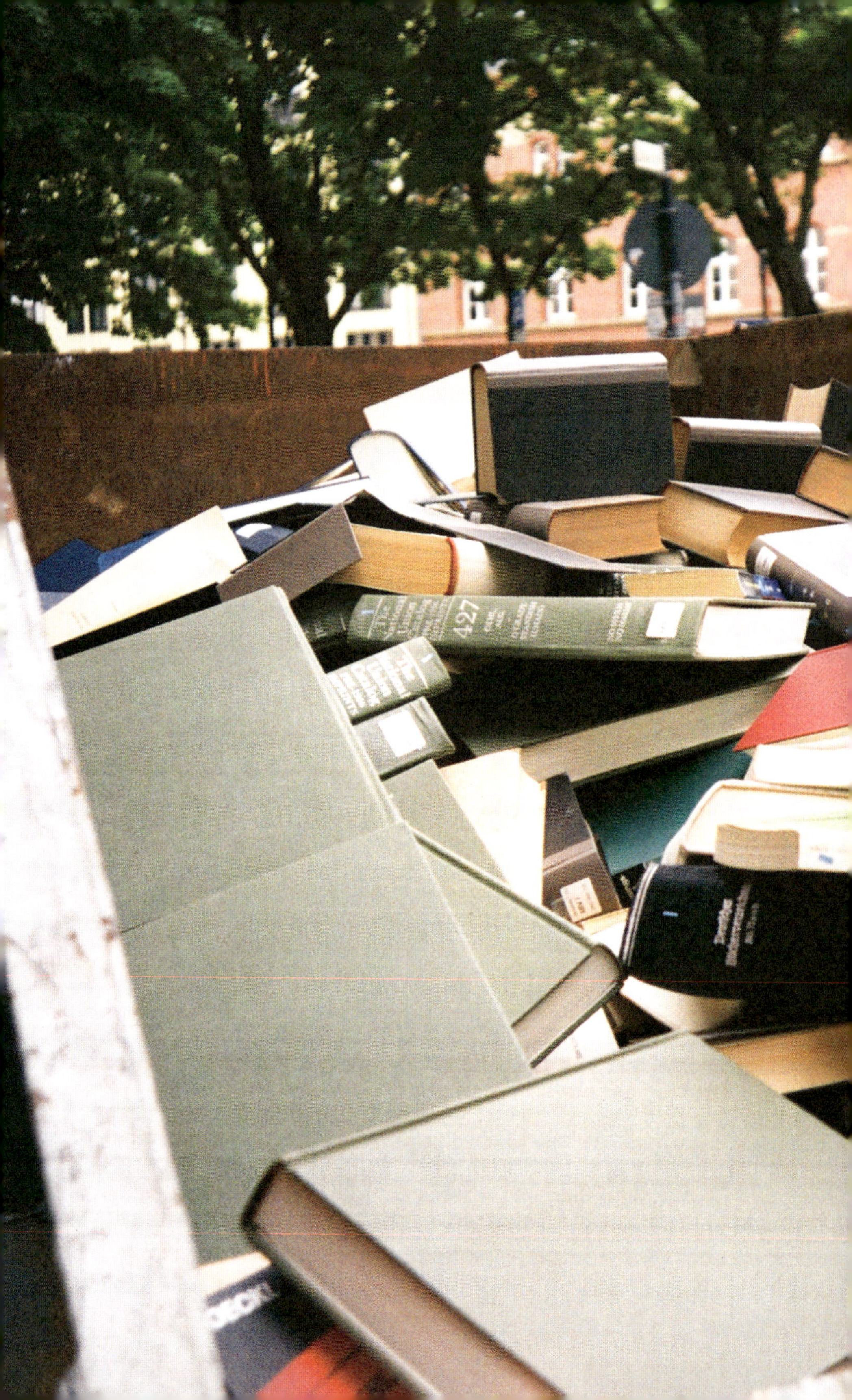
427